OUR HEARTS WERE
YOUNG AND GAY

BY
CORNELIA OTIS SKINNER
and
EMILY KIMBROUGH

DRAWINGS BY

alajálov.

DODD, MEAD & COMPANY
NEW YORK   1942

PRINTED IN THE UNITED STATES OF AMERICA
AMERICAN BOOK—STRATFORD PRESS, INC., NEW YORK

TO OUR MOTHERS

Lest the reader should be in any doubt, we wish to state that the incidents in this book are all true and the characters completely non-fictitious

CHAPTER 1

WE had been planning the trip for over a year. Pinching, scraping and going without sodas, we had salvaged from our allowances and the small-time jobs we each had found the preceding vacation the sum of $80.00, which was the cost of a minimum passage on a Canadian Pacific liner of the cabin class. Our respective families had augmented our finances by letters of credit generous enough to permit us to live for three months abroad if not in the lap of luxury, at least on the knees of comfort. For months we had been exchanging letters brimming over with rapturous plans and lyric anticipation and now June had really rolled around and the happy expectancy of the brides-to-be of that year had nothing on us.

It was settled we could meet in Montreal at whatever hotel it is that isn't the Ritz. I, clutching and occasionally kissing our steamship passage, was arriving from New York, Emily from Buffalo. That is, I hoped Emily was arriving. Emily's notions concerning geography, like some of her other notions, were enthusiastic but lacking in accuracy. Some weeks previous she had sent me a rhapsodic letter which ended with the alarming words, "I live for the moment when our boat pushes out from that dock in Winnipeg." I had written back in a panic and block letters stating, somewhat crushingly I thought, that the C.P.O. seldom sent its ships overland, that we were sailing from

Montreal, Province of Quebec, that the name of our vessel was the *Montcalm* and the date June 10th, the year of our Lord I shan't say which, because Emily and I have now reached the time in life when not only do we lie about our ages, we forget what we've said they are. Emily wrote back not to worry, darling, she had it all straight now. Moreover she was being motored up from Buffalo by friends who had been abroad often and who wouldn't dream of driving her to the wrong place. They would arrive sometime the afternoon of the 9th.

No such traveled and plutocratic friends offered to motor me to Canada, so I purchased an upper on the Montreal sleeper . . . a bit of misguided economy because once aboard the train I had to pay for another upper in order to accommodate my collection of luggage. The Skinners have ever, I believe, been respectable, God-fearing folk, but in those days my family made up for the lack of a skeleton in the closet by having extremely disreputable-looking luggage. Mother, the most exquisite of women, was fastidious to a degree when it came to the care of her clothes and mine, but she didn't care what she packed them in as long as the receptacle was clean. Consequently on this, the occasion of my first long trip on my own, she had, with loving care and acres of tissue-paper, stowed my effects in an assortment of containers that ranged from a canvas trunk Father had used when he played at Daly's, to a patent leather thing for hats that looked like a cover for a bass drum. There was a strapbound straw affair known for some reason as a "telescope," and various other oddments. I was made to carry my "good coat" (the one in which I traveled was my "every day") on a stout hanger in a voluminous green dress-bag which had a hole at the top and through that emerged the hook for hanging it up. It was a formidable looking contrivance and I used to glance nervously at that hook, half anticipat-

ing the sight of a human eye impaled upon it. In addition to all this there was that inevitable "box lunch for the trip." To be sure, the ride was only overnight but Mother, in whose veins flowed the blood of the pioneers, felt that no journey . . . even a visit to my aunt in Weehawken

. . . should be undertaken without a little supply of provender. I was a grown woman before I realized a Pullman berth need not necessarily be strewn with cracker-crumbs.

At the station I tried to rise above my luggage and bid my parents a worldly and somewhat indifferent good-bye. It was hard to get away with. Father, when it came to travel, went on the theory that I wasn't quite bright and as I look back on myself I don't think I was. Mother, despite my nineteen years and a lamentable determination to look like Theda Bara, still persisted in calling me "Baby." She kept reminding me to put my purse in my pillow, never to speak to any strange men, always to spread paper on "the seat" and to wire her if I arrived there safely. (She said nothing about wiring her if I didn't.) I quite expected her to pin my ticket on my blouse, tip the porter and tell him to make sure her little girl got off at Montreal. Often as we'd been separated, our partings were always emotional. Besides, this was my first flight from the home nest. I was going off on my own, whatever my own was. Mother cried a little and Father looked brave, but as if he never expected to meet me again in this world despite the fact that in all probability we'd be meeting again fairly shortly. They too were sailing, but on a different ship and from New York. They had no idea of cramping Emily's and my style, but they thought it just as well to be in the same hemisphere as we. They would be in England when we were and we might look them up if that wasn't too much of a strain on our independence.

Upon arrival in Montreal my emotions were indeed those of a little girl. It was my first experience of registering alone at a hotel and far from feeling emancipated and like Theda Bara, I felt frightened and forlorn and like Sara

Crewe in her worst circumstances. The clerk verified my
misgivings about myself by assigning me a room so high
up under the eaves I half expected pigeons to fly out of
the dresser. I had explained that "my friend" was arriving
. . . just when I couldn't say, but I hoped around noon.
This hope also was forlorn. When Emily says she'll arrive
around noon it can get so far around, it merges into noon
of the following day. I had a foreboding I'd spend hours
waiting for her and I was right. I was too shy to venture
forth alone in a strange town. Besides, I was afraid of not
being on hand for that significant moment when Emily
should arrive and our trip officially begin. The time
dragged along. I wrote some letters, studied bits of Baedeker and every fifteen minutes made certain my passport and letter of credit hadn't been stolen. This last
activity involved the opening up of a little contraption so
humiliating that the memory of it even now makes me turn
my attention rapidly to something else. Mother, who despite years of travel still cherished the colorful idea that any
journey beyond the boundaries of the United States was
beset with brigands and bandits, had harnessed about my
person an incredible object known as a "safety-pocket."
This was a large chamois purse that dangled at the knees
in the manner of a sporran and was attached in a sort of
block and tackle system of tape and buckle to an adjustable
belt around the waist. It was worn, supposedly inconspicu-
ously, under skirt and slip and I daresay in Mother's youthful and voluminously clad day which engendered this pru-
dent accessory, it flapped away subtly beneath yards of
broadcloth, watered-silk and batiste, and nobody was the
wiser. But in my youthful and more skimpy day, everybody was not only the wiser but the more bewildered.

The bag was heavily stuffed not only with a few British bank notes, but there had further been rammed into it my passport and letter of credit. I could never find a way of wearing it comfortably. If I arranged it so that it hung down in front, when I walked it would get to swinging, catching between my knees and making me go into a gait of an animated ice-hook. Hung in the rear it did even worse things, and when I sat still it had an unfortunate way of coming to rest either upon my upper leg or along my outer thigh giving me the outline of someone conceal-ing a squash. It was particularly complicated wearing it beneath the skin-tight exterior of my wardrobe. Those were the days of Gloria Swanson and Pola Negri, when people swooned over Ben Ali Haggin and some still quoted Kipling's "A fool there was" and it was my secret yearn-ing to look like that macabre specimen known as a "vamp." I went in for "slinky" dresses, high heels, long black ear-rings which I wore even when I played tennis, and perfume so strong my school buddies used to say they could smell me coming several seconds before they saw me. However, when it came to my traveling costume for this trip, I had added a quaint and varying note to my wardrobe. What flight of whimsey made me purchase a baby blue home-spun suit with a Norfolk jacket, heaven knows. To go with this I, who was anything but an out-door girl, had added a panama sports hat with a band around the crown, very severe, very Knox. I had even gone in for a pair of stout brown oxfords. I suppose the idea back of this bright little get-up was that when I wore it I shed, for the time be-ing, my Elinor Glyn tiger-skins and became the glowing, healthy American girl,—a type that would look well on a steamer. It was a pretty idea but not too successful. Being

unused to sensible heels I had a hard time with those oxfords and more than once found myself stepping with one
foot onto the extended sole of the other. Then the weather
or something shrunk the brim of my hat making it turn up
all the way around and I rather imagine I looked less like
Eleanor Sears than I did like Buster Brown. However, I
got into this costume now. I thought it would be appropri-
ate for meeting Emily. Besides, my safety-pocket wasn't as
noticeable under it as under more exotic garments.

At long last, Emily burst into the room. We were still
at an age when girl friends upon meeting after a long
absence, did a good deal of shrieking, and the sounds of
our greeting made ring whatever the welkin is. A bellboy,
barely discernible under Emily's mountain of luggage,
looked on with disgust until Emily became aware of his
presence and with the grand manner of royalty bestowing
Maundy money, doled him out a tip. His expression deepened from one of disgust into the epitome of sullen perse-
cution and with a suppressed snarl, he strode from the
room. As he turned, I caught a glimpse of the coin Emily
had handed him and, shocked by a sudden suspicion that
my friend might be what was then opprobriously known
as a "tight-wad," I ventured to ask, "Do you never tip
more than a penny?"

"A penny? Didn't you just see me give the boy a dollar?"

"No, dear, I just saw you give the boy a penny."

"Nonsense," she snorted, "I gave him the largest coin I
had. What's more, it was an English coin."

"Yes. And it was an English penny. Two cents in
America." Grabbing up her purse she rushed from the
room crying "Wait! I didn't mean it!" after the bellboy
who by now had vanished past a turn in the corridor. It

was some time before she returned. Knowing Emily and knowing that she attracts incident as blue serge attracts lint, I grew apprehensive. When finally she returned her face was the color of bortsch before they add the sour cream. It seems that after making good with the bellboy, she had wandered back counting her change, opened a door she for some vague reason thought was ours, and had acidly remarked "Well, I hope you feel better now" to what when she looked up proved to be an elderly gentleman completely nude. The experience had subdued her considerably and she said she thought she'd rather go back to Buffalo than any farther abroad. But I assured her that this was just one more proof of how broadening travel could be and, sitting her down, gave her a lesson in that branch of higher mathematics, British currency. I don't know what made me think I understood it myself. I still don't. But having spent the previous year in France, mine was the know-it-allness of the seasoned traveler. Emily hailed originally from Muncie, Indiana, and had never journeyed beyond American shores farther than Catalina Island, so during the first stages of our trip before she began finding out things for herself I passed up no opportunity for showing off.

She told me that what really had addled her had been the shock not so much of English money as the sight of me in that baby blue sports outfit. As a matter of fact her own traveling costume was not without its element of originality. It, too, was tweed . . . that flecked variety known as "pepper and salt." She had designed it herself and her mother's dressmaker had run it up. There was a skirt which was innocuous enough; with it, however, went not a jacket but a loose, rather billowing cape of the same material,

lined with orange taffeta. What topped everything off, and in more ways than one, was her hat, which was also of the same tweed cloth and also run up by local talent. It had a small brim and a soft, folded crown that was meant to fit

snugly to the head. Through some oversight the folds hadn't been stitched together and as a result, at the slightest breeze or toss of her head, the crown would open out like a collapsible drinking cup and rise to its full length of a good yard in the air. And there it would stay unless I found a chance to whisper to her, "Your hat's up again," at which she would grab hold of the clownish peak and crush the sections back into place. Emily, who usually looked neat and chic, in this cape and Robin-Goodfellow hat seemed curiously Shakespearean and that was the last effect she'd had in mind when she designed the ensemble. The fact that Emily should suddenly turn up looking Shakespearean at the same moment I turned up looking like an adult version of the Little Colonel is just one more proof that at that age, you never can tell.

Those distinguished friends who had driven Emily from Buffalo had asked us to dine with them at the Ritz and we felt the occasion called for a bath and a change of clothes. Neither of us is the modest type of girl who disrobes behind doors or struggles out of her garments under cover of a slip. I knew the moment was at hand when Emily would see me in my shame and nakedness and attired only in that safety-pocket. Knowing the sight would shock her I thought it wise to break the information to her gently.

"Emily," I began, "I think you ought to know. It's very unfortunate but I have to . . . to wear something. . . ."

Emily cut me short.

"Stop!" she cried. "I've been wondering for days how to tell you." And with a dramatic gesture she swished up her skirt. There dangling between her legs like a gourd from a vine was the twin of my ghastly appendage.

"Mother fastened one on me too," she groaned. "She says it's the only way I'll keep my money safe."

The discovery that Emily, too, was the victim of the same motherly precaution heartened me a good deal. I loved Emily dearly but I also admired her to a point when I had occasionally to remind myself that after all she was born in Muncie, to keep from being a bit over-awed by her. I felt I was definitely her inferior and hoped she wouldn't find it out. Her luggage was very smart and in comparison mine looked more than ever like the gleanings of a gypsy camp. With the possible exception of that "pepper and salt" outfit, she dressed simply but smartly and it made me think my long earrings and attempts to resemble

Theda Bara were more spectacular than chic. Then, too, Emily read a lot. She was familiar with Huneker and she knew all about the James Brothers . . . not Jesse and Frank but the more literary Henry and William, while I still had a secret letch for Ethel M. Dell. Most impressive of all, she had been engaged and after announcing it, had broken it off. At nineteen I hadn't thought of being en-

gaged . . . that is, I had but nobody else had. The discov
ery that she too wore a safety-pocket brought her nearer
my level.

We bathed, changed from our curious traveling attire
into our best crêpe marocain dresses and went to the Ritz,
where Emily's friends blew us to a lavish feast. We each
put on an act for the benefit of the other, trying to behave
as if quail and champagne at the Ritz were merely the
equivalent of a banana-split and hot chocolate with marsh-
mallow whip at the Bryn Mawr Cottage Tea Room. I'm
afraid we didn't get away with it. The champagne gave
us away. I had lived in Paris for a year but had never
drunk anything more giddy than vin ordinaire thinned
with Evian. Champagne was as unknown to me as mari-
juana, but I tried to be as casual about it as an old Deauville rip. Emily, who was descended from a long line of
Indiana teetotalers, took her first sip of demon alcohol
with the bravura of Eve biting into the apple. This was
when she discovered that champagne makes her slightly
deaf. Its effect upon me was to make me look distant and
sad and I hoped everyone would think I had had an un-
happy love affair.

It was a gay repast. Our host, George Field, a delightful
individual with a mad imagination, spent a good part of the
evening giving Emily a few helpful hints on ocean travel.
He said it would be advisable for her to learn to tell ship's
time because on a vessel bells rang every quarter hour but
if you asked an officer what time had struck, he would
put his finger to his lips and say, "Sh! We're not allowed
to tell." It was part of the discipline of the British merchant marine. Then, too, she must be ready for passenger
drill. Stray mines from the last war (this was in the early

ill menacing the shipping lanes and crews and
d to be prepared for emergencies. Any day
ight take it into his head to shout "Kimbrough
to the boats." and she'd have to leap to her station in a
lifeboat and row spiritedly for ten minutes or so.

"Of course," he went on, "crossing the northern route
you're certain to have the added fun of fog and icebergs.
You'll be passing the Banks of Newfoundland, a most
picturesque experience. In thick weather (which is practically constant) you'll be aware of a curious hollow noise.
That will be the barking of the Newfoundland dogs who
are trained to sit on the Banks and warn ships of the treacherous shoals." He went on to explain that Canadian ships
didn't have to start out with any ice supply. The U.S. Ice
Patrol radioed the position of the nearest and handiest berg,
the vessel pulled up alongside and the crew, equipped with
ice-picks and buckets, leaned over the railing and chipped
off enough ice to replenish the refrigerators. The passengers, provided they were good, were allowed to chip, too,
sometimes, as part of the deck sports. He fabricated even
wilder nautical fantasies and we all laughed heartily.

All, that is, except Emily who didn't actually believe
him but who thought that as in the case of a number of
things, thirteen at table, for instance, you never could tell
and maybe we oughtn't laugh. The Kimbroughs of Indiana
are not the breed that engendered John Paul Jones, and
even now Emily takes to ships and sea-faring as a duck
takes to Death Valley. A ferry crossing from the Central
of New Jersey to Desbrosses Street hurls her into a panic.
After dinner when we had returned to our hotel and were
preparing for our last sleep on dry land she said, and for
some reason said it quite accusingly, "Why, I don't even

like a trip on a Boston swan-boat!"

Next morning we woke up in a state of elation. June 10th had actually dawned and the world hadn't come to an end. As we dressed Emily sang an Ethelbert Nevin song that began "A brave good morn to thee, my love" which was all about some girl getting married to somebody else and didn't have much bearing on events at hand and I sang, "This is my lucky day," which I thought did, even if it was less refined. We gulped some coffee, packed and counted over our luggage for a bit but gave it up because each time we came out with a different amount. Somehow we got to the dock and there actually moored alongside, smoke pouring from her smokestack, the blue peter fluttering at her mainmast, was the *Montcalm*, a real live ship, not just the paper diagram we'd been mulling over for six months. It was a momentous occasion and we were at that happy age when we felt momentous occasions should be reacted to with emotional respect. Oblivious to the jostling crowd, we stood gazing at the prosaic decks of the modest cabin-class liner, dewy-eyed, clutching each other, dropping things and holding up a line of less sensitive passengers.

The Fields saw us on board, George continuing to elucidate to Emily matters of maritime education. The winches confused her and he explained that they were part of the captain's machine, a sort of tatting affair, on which he turned out those well-known "knots per hour," while the passengers stood about admiringly and bet on the ship's daily run. Again we laughed and again Emily half believed him. A brass gong sounded and Emily emitted her first apprehensive "What's that?" an interrogation she was to repeat at short intervals clear across the Atlantic.

The Fields bade us Godspeed and went ashore and not long after that the gangplank was hoisted clear. The foghorn let forth its shattering but beautiful bark and then slowly, proudly, unbelievably the little steamer moved from the dock, backed into the St. Lawrence, turned her nose toward the east and headed for England. Again we clutched each other and I guess we cried a little,—certainly we tried to. Then I got efficient and suggested we ought perhaps to go locate our places in the dining room, but Emily said she preferred to stand by the rail and be emotional, so I went below trying to create an impression of being a seasoned, cultivated traveler. The impression apparently didn't take with the Chief Steward because after one look at me, he allotted us two cards for First Service (Second was the chic meal) at the table of an obscure officer, the sort who, on a three-class ship, would head a table in student-steerage. By the time I came up on deck Emily had completed her emotional orgy and was engaged in animated conversation with a monocled officer in a swank uniform with a lot of gold braid and a strip across his chest like a color-chart. The gorgeous creature was of course British, in fact so much so, his speech came from him with an effort almost apoplectic. Emily, not to be outdone, had launched forth in a novel accent of her own, one which, it later developed, she used whenever she conversed with English people and felt ill-at-ease, which was whenever she conversed with English people. She broadened her "a's" and made a few sounds on the "metter of fect" order, but Indiana's honest "r's" still clung like burrs to a sheep dog, which was probably why, as I came up, the officer was asking her if she was from Wales by any chance. Emily said no, not by any chance and turned to introduce her dazzling conquest. It was clear she had no idea of his name but the glitter of gold braid and brass buttons made her feel she should mention his rank.

"This is my friend Miss Skinner, Cap . . . er . . . Command . . . er . . . Admir . . . " The glorious creature put an end to her floundering by barking out something that sounded like "Cracker" but was probably Mac-Gregor, adjusted his monocle and resumed his talk with Emily, which appeared to be on a very cultural plane. Emily, who somehow didn't think that he'd know about Muncie or even Buffalo, had given as her general address the entire continent of North America. He was telling her that he himself came from Chester and Emily was nostalgically saying: "Oh yes, the old Walled town of Chester" as if, except for what she'd read about Chester in Baedeker the previous evening, she had any remote familiarity with the name unless as applied to a white Indiana hog. The gentleman was obviously impressed for he produced from some hidden cranny in that sausage-tight jacket some snapshots of his wife and what he called "nippers." This I felt had every earmark of the beginnings of a guilty but definitely distinguished situation for Emily. I whispered that I guessed I was *de trop* (pronouncing "trop" to rhyme with "drop" to be witty) and with admirable tact I slunk away, ordered our deck chairs and sat in one with a book which I didn't read. I have never been able to concentrate on a book on shipboard. People keep passing and no matter whether they turn out to be nothing more exciting than a deckhand, I have to look up, maybe with some subconscious and optimistic hope that sometime I'll be gazing into the eyes of Prince Charming. Then if for a space nobody passes, I have to look out at the sea to make sure it's still there. Besides, on this occasion I was too excited to read. Our trip of independence had begun. There were no parents, no chaperones to cramp our style, whatever that was. Before us was something I liked to think of as "Life" or better still, the "Beau Monde," a bright pageant of characters and situations culled from the pages of Scott Fitzgerald and the royalty section of the London *Tatler*. Who knew what delectable adventures awaited us? Who indeed? Even now little Emily, radiant and tremulous, was embarking on what might blossom into romance. I recalled the snapshots of the poor wife and nippers back in Chester and thought how conscience-stricken Emily would feel . . . and how pleased. I wondered if there were another married man on board whose home *I* might wreck in the interim between Montreal and Liverpool. Emily had obviously bagged the most distinguished but then I wasn't choosey. I wasn't aiming for anyone high up in the Admiralty. Any presentable man would serve. My reverie was cut short by Emily, who plopped into the chair beside me looking anything but radiant and tremulous. Moreover, she appeared to be quite cross with me. The only times Emily and I ever became unpleasant with one another were when we found ourselves in awkward situations of our own making. As she said nothing, I asked tentatively:

"What have you done with your Admiral?"

"I haven't done anything with him," she snapped. "And he isn't an Admiral."

"Oh."

There was a pause.

"He isn't even an officer."

"Oh?"

There was another pause and then the truth came out.

"He's the leader of the ship's band. And it isn't even the orchestra. It's some sort of band that plays in the morning to let you know that bouillon's ready."

The only reply to this was another "Oh" and to avoid further embarrassment, we resorted to our books. I did venture to enquire if he might not turn out to be a problem but she said, "No, I didn't give him any encouragement." I tactfully avoided any further mention of the subject and after a bit Emily grew less cross at me. It was a heavenly day. The engines chugged soothingly, the air was balmy and beyond the railing, hazy and serene, the tidy shores of the St. Lawrence slipped past like a water color on an endless scroll. The books in our hands sank supine on our stomachs and our eyes became glazed.

We were roused by the blast of a bugle played cacophonously in our ear by a young steward who must have been studying the instrument in six easy lessons and hadn't progressed beyond the fourth. At the sound Emily leapt to her feet like a salmon up-stream, pale but controlled, and said:

"Our life preservers are in our cabin, aren't they?"

"Yes," I said. "Why?"

"Why? Didn't you hear that trumpet? It means something, doesn't it?"

"Certainly," I answered. "It means the First Service for lunch is ready." And I yawned to show what an old sea-dog I was, to be sure. Then I remembered that we were in the First Service and we went below.

Our table (it was off to one side near the swing-doors where stewards in order to get past had to graze our heads with their trays) held about ten people in addition to the officer who sat at the head. He was a grim individual who said nothing. As a matter of fact, all ten of us said nothing and I began to feel I was back in school at the Latin table. Eventually the rather nice looking man on Emily's right asked if he might trouble her for the salt and she burbled her reassurance that it was anything but trouble. Then to the left of me an English lad with a beef-steak complexion and a good many prominent teeth uttered in my general direction that the weather was jolly decent and I agreed rather strenuously, yes, wasn't it, and he said, yes, it was, and that stretch of ice was broken.

At the outset we tried to act as if our interest in men was purely academic, but soon gave up the pretense as too much of a strain. Emily's companion was named Mr. Blot. He was correct, good looking and said little. Reflecting now upon Mr. Blot I imagine that this was because he had little to say. However, discussing him later that day in the privacy of our cabin, we came to the more romantic conclusion that he was the strong silent type. My buddy, the one with the teeth, was anything but silent and I also suspect anything but strong. But he was pleasant, wore pants and was unattached. Moreover, as further proof of his desirability, he presented me with what was left of a box of Page and Shaw because he was afraid that when we got on the high seas he might be sick.

Our cabin, at minimum fare, was an inside cubicle, so far below decks it appeared to be resting just above the keel. If we had some vague idea of spending the afternoon there unpacking, one glance at it informed us that nothing could be unpacked in it with the possible exception of our toothbrushes. Our luggage, piled in hopeless confusion, covered the only three square feet of floor space. We tried stowing some of it under the berth but it wouldn't go, due to the presence of some bulky obstruction that felt like a body but turned out to be life preservers. Emily, who was the apprehensive type, said we'd better keep those accessible because you never knew, so what time we remained in the place we moved about amid and on top of our luggage in the manner of hikers crossing a boulder-field. To approach the basin we either leaned over a tall innovation valise or sat gingerly on the edge of another bit of impedimenta and when it came to brushing the teeth, aimed optimistically in the direction of the drain.

Unpacking being out of the question, we left our effects stored in suitcases like the wares of an itinerant lace merchant and climbed up several layers of deck to more spacious regions. It was doubtless Emily's prohibition ancestry that made her instinctively recoil at the sign "Main Saloon" but she relaxed when all that met her eye was a large drawing room full of respectable and elderly couples and the usual scattering of horrid little children. We found the writing room and a couple of unoccupied desks and we set to work using up as many free postcards as we could think of people upon whom to inflict them. My list of friends being considerably shorter than Emily's, I left her busily repeating "Dearest So-and-So. This is our ship. X doesn't mark our cabin because it's below the water. We're having a glorious . . . etc., etc." and went on deck. The day was sparkling and I leaned on the railing taking the sort of deep, brave breaths people who lean on railings think it their duty to take, and in a state of happy vacuity, watched the scenery slip past. Gradually I became aware that the scenery was no longer slipping. It was staying perfectly motionless. The engines were still pounding, if anything, harder than ever. Looking down over the side I saw that water was passing the ship, only it was going the wrong way. Also it was suddenly very muddy. People began to gather along the rail studying alternately the stationary shoreline and the churning brown water. The words "gone aground," "run into shoals" or just plain "STUCK" sounded out ominously. The English lad with the teeth came up beside me and announced cheerfully "Well, we've caught bottom" as if it were a record sail fish. "All right for a time but when the tide goes down she'll settle onto rocks."

"Is that bad?" I croaked.

"Probably means a few large holes in the hull. She'll list badly . . . may even capsize. Cheer-o" and he hurried off to spread gladness among others.

By now everyone was rushing out onto the deck . . . everyone but Emily. I went in search of her and found her the sole occupant of the writing room penning a blissful letter to her family telling them how much she loved the ship.

"Emily," I began, breaking the information to her as gently as possible. "I have something unfortunate to tell you."

"Mm?" she grunted, not looking up.

"Emily dear, I hate to bother you but we're shipwrecked."

Again she grunted and failed to look up. I thought perhaps the news had been too much for her.

"Didn't you hear what I said?"

"Yeah," she replied, still writing. "You said we were shipwrecked."

"But we are. We're aground. Don't you care?"

"Oh, go away!" she snorted. This was evidently to

her just another George Field whimsey.

"All right if you want to stay here and drown!" and I strode dramatically outside. The shore was still stationary but one side of the deck was perceptibly lower than the other. There was an atmosphere of suppressed excitement about. Seamen were appearing in doorways and disappearing down hatches and ladders. Officers with "for King and Country" expressions were hastening to the bridge. One could hear pumps being worked. A lifeboat was swung out on the davits, then a second and a third. Apprehensive passengers began making muttering sounds like the crowd extras in Julius Caesar. The tide was rapidly going down and I waited for the happy moment when the steel plates of the hull would start caving in. The side which was at a lower angle became even more so. The ship's barber, an assistant purser and the official photographer mingled with the passengers reassuring the more jittery ones that it was "just temp'ry"—as if they knew! The engines were now working themselves into a threatened angina trying to shove us out of the mud. At one moment the ship gave a little shudder and leap in a modified imitation of the *Hesperus*, then settled down on one side as if for a long nap. Exactly one second later Emily, blanched and wild-eyed, shot out of the companionway like a bat out of the Carlsbad caverns. She grabbed my arm and pointed at the motionless farmhouse we'd all been watching for at least an hour.

"Look!" she cried. "We're stuck! The boat's tipping over! Don't you think we ought to tell the captain?"

CHAPTER 2

THE *Montcalm* was stuck fast and seemed to have given up the struggle. The engines had stopped and the only sound from below was the desperate chugging of the pumps—which wasn't particularly comforting. The list had settled into a static pose like the Tower of Pisa. Everybody collected along the rail that was down, probably because it was easiest, and glared at the water in indignation. Emily said she was going to start doing her bit by persuading people to go over to the other side of the ship and maybe that would right it. But Mr. Blot, who at that moment came up lighting his pipe and looking like the embodiment of gentlemanly morale, explained that that wouldn't do much good. To Mr. Blot, who went through life an unconscious example of the *raison d'être* of the British Empire, a shipwreck was merely one of the many things to be ignored. His was a calming influence. The fact that he was struggling painfully to light his pipe was in itself reassuring. He would hardly be taking all that trouble if he believed there were any immediate possibility of its being extinguished. In his quiet opinion the ship was "definitely fast" (he meant stuck, not speedy) and we might expect to remain there for days. We asked him if we were going to tip over and he said he thought, on the whole, not. And with that meagre hope he left us to carry on.

Some tugs came alongside and tried giving us a few helpful shoves with as much effect as a motorcycle helping a sand-bogged Greyhound bus. Emily grew hourly more apprehensive and even I, old salt that I wasn't, didn't feel particularly happy. Toward four o'clock a river steamer came up to "stand-by"—a horrid term. The sight of it grimly waiting there to pick up splashing passengers alarmed Emily to such a degree she couldn't even look at it. I tried to be encouraging.

"But, Emily," I remonstrated. "What if we do capsize? See how close we are to shore! You could swim there easily."

"No, I couldn't." Emily had learned to swim, under protest, at Bryn Mawr, and then only because unless she swam the length of the pool twice, she couldn't get out of the freshman class. "I can swim only fifty strokes if I count and I'm in no condition to count."

The afternoon passed and so did a number of other ships and by dinner time there was nothing to do but go eat it, even if it wasn't very appetizing to eat at an angle. The lad with the rush of teeth to the fore blew us to a bottle of *vin* which was pretty *ordinaire* but which helped somewhat. The captain being occupied with the pumps or something, the purser made a speech to the cheery effect that we were not to become alarmed (for those of us who had, he offered no solution) that the vessel wasn't ready quite just yet for Davy Jones's Locker (humor not very successful) and that by morning they expected to have some good news for us. (Emily muttered, "Probably a bouncing boy.") He went on to say that everything would continue as per "shed-ule" and that the first night get-together dance would be held as usual. Our table companions seemed to think this a ripping good idea and Emily and I, to show that we too could "carry on," said we'd go. The festivity took place in a canvas-enclosed area of deck B where a steward had strung up some giddy paper lanterns and an enterprising cabin boy had strewn the floor with a miniature blizzard of what looked like Lux flakes—some sort of preparation for turning bare, holystoned planks into polished ballroom hardwood. The orchestra (not conducted by Emily's admiral) played nothing newer than "Dardanella" and excerpts from "The Chocolate Soldier," and a handful of us tried to pretend it was fun. My young friend of the teeth said he for one thought the music was jolly decent. I could agree with him only in half. It was certainly decent, but hardly jolly. Attendance was poor. People on a grounded, listing ship aren't in a gala mood. Moreover the deck, thanks to those Lux flakes, was dangerously slippery. It was like dancing on an icy ski-tow. What few couples were courageous enough to try it soon gave it up. We stuck at it only because there wasn't anything else to do. Mr. Blot twirled Emily about with all the animation of one of Mme. Tussaud's more refined figures, while my friend bounced me about keeping eager and energetic time to something that wasn't at all what the music had in mind. Spinning or hopping, we would manage to gain the summit of the sloping floor, then, like tangled-up skiers we'd whoosh down to the other side, the railing being all that kept us from continuing on into the waters of the St. Lawrence. It was hard work and I grew breathless and slightly dizzy. Gradually I became aware that something soft and strange was bumping against my knees and the portion of my legs that might be called "upper" having not quite graduated into thighs. At first I thought it had something to do with my partner's knees. But I couldn't fathom how he was doing it or why, or what gave his knees that padded, detached quality. He in turn began glancing downward uneasily and I realized that something was, in all probability, hitting him too. Then, with a wave of horror, it dawned upon me what was happening. That

mortifying safety-pocket of mine had got swaying and was rhythmically and indiscriminately thudding first against my limbs then against those of the mystified young man. It was all extremely awful and I began to wish fervently the boat would choose that moment in which to capsize. Any explanation was out of the question. To confess that under my modest skirt I harbored such an object would have been unthinkable. There was no alternative but to say that I thought maybe I'd better stop now and he agreed with alacrity. We left the dance floor somewhat abruptly and at the precise moment in which Emily and Mr. Blot also walked off. Mr. Blot was looking perplexed and Emily was red and seemingly on the verge of tears. Emily's sporran, too, had caught the spirit of things and had likewise started boops-a-daisying. We excused ourselves in haste and fled to our cabins where we divested our persons of those abominations. Had our mothers been within range we would doubtless have hurled them at the poor well-intentioned darlings. I often wonder if Mr. Blot and that toothy lad ever got together and if so what awful conclusions they could have reached.

We thought it wise to stay out of sight until the shock factor of the incident had worn off. It was late and being tired, we decided we might as well take a chance on going to bed. Our cabin steward assured us we were in no danger and we asked him how *he* knew and he grinned and said, "Listen for the siren. If anything goes wrong you'll 'ear it. You might keep your body-finches 'andy too."

"How are we going to hear a siren way down here in this submarine coop?" Emily muttered. "Listen for sirens! We've no more chance of hearing any sirens than Ulysses's men after they got their ears stopped up. And what was that about keeping a bull-finch handy?"

"A body-finch." I was again the offensive seasoned traveler. "That's what they call a life preserver."

"Why don't they call it by its real name?" Emily, all Indiana rampant, tugged hers out from behind the piles of luggage and then for a long time she studied the framed notice on the wall that showed the way to adjust it and the location of one's lifeboat. Ours was #6 on the port side and that didn't help her any. Port to her was something you drank on special occasions like Thanksgiving and when I told her it meant "left as you face forward," she said how was she to know where forward was when the ship wasn't moving. Then she laid her life jacket on the foot of her berth, carefully opening it out like a bed-spread.

With admirable unselfishness she had insisted upon sleeping in the upper bunk and after a bit of polite protesting I said, oh, very well, which proved to be a mistake, because she neither slept nor did she remain in the bunk for more than fifteen minutes at a stretch. During the night her nervousness increased. She kept getting down and creeping to the stateroom door which she would open with caution but considerable creaking, and peer apprehensively down the passageway at the end of which was an open port-hole. Then, making certain that as yet no sea water was pouring in she'd return to bed, only to repeat the action again a few minutes later. Between sallies she made curious swishing noises with the bedclothes and when I asked her what she was doing she said *Sh!* she was just practicing swimming strokes and for me please to go to sleep. I might have obliged if each time she descended from above and at the precise moment when I was about to doze off, she hadn't stepped squarely onto my face. Not wishing to disturb me by turning on a light, in complete darkness she would grope around with her bare foot until she encountered an object solid enough to bear her weight. The object invariably proved to be my face and when I protested she said she didn't know why I slept with my face out so far anyway.

Next morning at breakfast we were told that all passengers would be taken off on tenders and that we must be packed and ready to leave by noon, and by eight that evening the only palpable results of the idea were the fact that we were still sitting in our traveling clothes clinging to passports, handbags and forlorn hopes. Everyone was afraid to leave the vicinity of the purser's office for fear of losing out on the latest rumor. I did, however, venture as far as the wireless room. It occurred to me that my parents were by now on the high seas and remembering that the little daily ship's newspaper carries all the latest maritime reports, I was afraid they might read news of the *Montcalm* being aground and come to melodramatic conclusions. So I wired, "Don't worry. Everything will be all right." My father later told me he received this odd communication while walking about the deck in a state of anything but worry. He thought at first it must be in code. But Mother read it and said it boded no good. (They never did hear about the *Montcalm* and during the remainder of their voyage they were in a state of bewildered uneasiness.)

After sending my wire I returned to Emily and we waited and waited for hours. Then a government boat came alongside and some C.P.O. officials boarded our derelict. They strode into the main saloon, spread a lot of lists and diagrams out on a table and announced they were there to book passages on whatever other ships might be sailing within the next few days and all hell broke loose. People nudged, pushed, bruised and gouged one another in their frenzy to get near the table. It never occurred to anyone to line us up alphabetically but eventually a near panic was averted by some level-headed stewards who took it upon themselves to form us into line. It was a line so long it had to double back on itself a number of times as in a football snake dance, and since each person fortunate enough to gain the desk took at least fifteen minutes to adjust his or her tickets, it moved with the celerity of a very old glacier.

What wasn't like a glacier was the room, which was stifling hot. "There isn't a breath of air in this saloon," Emily gasped. She could never bring herself to say that word without glancing over her shoulder, possibly to see if anyone from Muncie were around. It seemed needless for both of us to suffocate so we decided to take ten minute turns, one holding the place in the line and the other going out on deck for air. The system revived us to a certain degree but after two hours we were still removed from our goal by several laps. Our hopes of ever securing berth on another vessel dwindled. The clock pointed to eleven-thirty. It was my turn to hold our place, Emily's to be relieved. And that she should have been relieved at that particular time is just one more manifestation of the fact that things happen to Emily which never happen to anyone else. On the same instant in which she emerged from the saloon onto the upper deck there came from down over the side the sound of a heavy splash, and a moment later the voice of the watch calling out the colorful words "Man overboard!" Then a second voice, less colorful but more practical, shouted, "Throw him a deck chair." The deck chairs were ranged in folded stacks along the inner wall and Emily rushed to secure one. Emily, who is of a romantic temperament, is rather prone to visualize big moments to come. At this point, she later told me, she was summoning up a picture of herself on the bridge with the captain. The rest of the passengers (myself humbly included) were grouped admiringly below looking up at a little ceremony in which the captain made a speech about her presence of mind in an emergency and by way of dramatic conclusion pinned a memento on her. The deck chair was heavy and awkward. Bits of it kept opening out, pinching her hands and ankles. She managed to drag it to the rail, however, and as she struggled to hoist it, that vision of the captain's memento turned gloriously into the Carnegie medal. With herculean effort she heaved the unwieldy object to the top and pushed. Due to the darkness she could scarcely see what she was doing, but she heard.

There was a crack like the sound of a torpedo banged on the sidewalk on the Fourth of July. She leaned over the railing and peered down. A searchlight was now flashing from the bridge. It was all too clear what had happened. The chair was wobbling about on the surface of the water but there was no trace of the man. If she had practiced for months, her marksmanship could not have been more perfect. She had landed her missile squarely on the top of his head. There was a lot of running on the part of the crew, a lifeboat was lowered and a number of us from the main saloon hastened outside. From the general buzz of conversation I gathered what had happened and in some strange flash of intuition I suspected Emily of having some unfortunate connection with it. She was standing apart from the others, looking as if a deck chair had fallen on her too. I went right up to her (to this day she says she thinks it was a most curious thing for me to have done) and said in a low voice, "Did you do that?" Emily managed to gasp out "Yes" and I said, "Well, we'll just keep on walking." I knew then how it felt to be sheltering a fugitive from justice. It felt awful. Silently we walked around the deck, returned to the scene of the crime and with expressions of Raphael's cherubs asked what the commotion was about. We were told that a wretched immigrant who was being deported had seized the opportunity, while the ship had stopped, to jump overboard and make for shore and freedom, but that some crazed passenger had hit him with a deck chair and sunk him. Steeling myself I asked if he were dead. Emily couldn't speak and I thought we ought to know the worst. The reply was no, only unconscious, probably a case of concussion. After being assured the man would live, Emily decided she wouldn't feel right the rest of her life unless she gave herself up and told the captain she'd done it. We found our way to the bridge and bravely asked for the captain, who for some reason agreed to see us. There was no crowd below looking on with admiration and he pinned no memento on Emily but he was extremely kind and cheered her by saying her action had merely made it easier for the seamen to haul the man back on board. The doctor had administered first aid and he was going to be all right. As a parting shot he added that anyway he didn't consider her responsible—which struck us as a dubious morsel of comfort.

Remembering we hadn't yet secured our passage on another ship, we returned to the saloon, which by now was deserted except for an unfeeling purser's assistant who told us the agents had disposed of the last inch of space on every available ship and we'd have to wait till we got to Quebec to see what the main office could do for us. We asked him when would we get to Quebec and he said, "That's just the question," which seemed to us just what we'd asked him and like the beginning of a round. We went to bed feeling strangely marooned.

By now they'd transferred the cargo onto lighters, the oil supply had in some way been syphoned into a tanker and the fresh water dumped out. The ship was considerably lightened and when the tide came in at three A.M., with a heave and a wallow which again brought Emily out of the upper berth and onto my face, the *Montcalm* lifted off the rocks and slowly, at an angle like an invalid with a droop to one side, a bevy of attendant little tugs fussing, nosing and encouraging her, began staggering down stream.

By morning we were moving along at quite a clip, although with a list which made one instinctively lean in the opposite direction. In spite of the damaged bottom it looked as if we were going to reach Quebec after all. Then arose the question of once having reached it what was to become of us. No one told us anything except that there was apparently no room for us anywhere. We might have to stay in Quebec for days and that wasn't our idea of a trip abroad. We certainly hadn't saved up for over a year just to squander it all on one riotous excursion to Ste. Anne de Beaupré. Then suddenly, blessedly I remembered that near Quebec was a tiny French Canadian village called Les Eboulements where Miss Mary spent her summers. Heavenly, incredible Miss Mary! Her other name was Mrs. Charles B. Dudley and she hailed from the Main Line (Philadelphia, of course). She was my mother's most intimate friend. She was also my guardian. That is, she was the person to whom Mother always wrote before undertaking a journey asking that in case she, Mother, were the victim of a wreck please to be kind to little Cornelia. What better time to make use of a guardian? To be sure I was the one who was the victim of the wreck, but despite my height and my nineteen years I felt very "little Cornelia." I guess it was only within the security of my immediate family circle that I enjoyed that independent Theda Bara feeling. I sent her a wireless saying we were barely making

port on a rapidly sinking vessel and were about to be
turned loose on the streets of Quebec without a passage
to our name and was there anything she could do about it.
The wireless was expensive but under the circumstances
we decided it was worth it. By noon the Plains of Abraham
hove in view and by way of distraction we tried to recall
our history and wondered lugubriously if it was Montcalm
who perished there . . . or Wolfe. We had received no
answering message from Miss Mary. I reached the gloomy
conclusion that either she wasn't at Les Eboulements or
she didn't care for me any more.

The tugs shoved and snorted and the *Montcalm*, listing
more than ever, rounded the last bend in the river, slowed
up, backed water and made the end of the dock. All passengers left the ship the moment the gangplank was down,
and I may say they left more in the traditional manner of
rats than human beings. Two steamers, the *Chicago* and
the *Regina*, were moored alongside with steam up, waiting
to take on everybody, everybody except Emily and me.
We found ourselves on the dock amid a pandemonium of
milling, hysterical individuals, who were trying to locate
their luggage, the steamship agents and strayed members of
their families. We stood for a time helplessly looking on.
The porters were all busy and paid no attention to us. We
were at an age when porters, with an eye to bigger business, never paid any attention to us anyway. We collected
our hand luggage from various widely divergent regions of
the shed where bits of it had been scattered here and there,
and looked frantically about for our trunks. Suddenly
Emily emitted a wail and pointed. There they were in a
great rope net being hoisted onto the *Chicago*. We rushed
to the edge of the pier and screamed loudly and in unison

that we weren't going on the *Chicago*. Nobody paid the slightest attention to us, and our trunks were ruthlessly dumped onto the deck along with a collection of others which were fast disappearing down a hatch. We raced onto the ship and managed to arrive on the forward deck just as they were about to follow the other baggage into the hold. We shrieked that those were ours and to please give them back to us, whereupon a stevedore flung them at our feet and went away leaving us to retrieve them as best we could. Nobody would help us. The hour for the departure of the *Chicago* was drawing near and we were in a panic for fear we'd get caught. There was nothing to do but haul them away ourselves. Desperation must give one strength at times. I don't know how we did it. Certainly Emily isn't strong and I have been known to buckle under after carrying a typewriter one block. But puffing, tugging and bent in two, we managed to yank the great objects to the chute, where we slid them to the dock.

Every porter had by now disappeared and we were obliged to continue like Volga boatmen the entire length of the quay. We were dirty, hot and miserable. Nobody seemed to care whether or not we had trunks or a porter or a permanent curvature. We didn't try to hide the fact that we were sniffling audibly and that suddenly, in spite of our chagrin over those safety-pockets, we wanted our mothers.

Then out of the gloom there burst upon us the vision of a C.P.O. official and to us he looked a good deal the way Perseus must have looked to Andromeda. He came right up and informed us that we were the two young ladies he was out to get, and as he was quite handsome and distinguished, that was all right by us too. We were to go at once to that

swank hostelry, the Château Frontenac, and stay there at
the company's expense until the *Empress of France* sailed
in eight days. The other ships were small and overcrowded
and by waiting we'd get better accommodations on a lux-
ury liner for the same fare. We must of course say nothing
to the other passengers about it. Why we should thus have
been singled out we never knew, but we asked no questions. Someone had come to our rescue. We had an impulse
to fling our arms about his well-tailored shoulders and sob
"Daddy" but we were afraid that might make him change
his mind. In our wonderment we were still clutching the
handles of our trunks. He told us gently that we could let
those go now, he'd see that all our things got safely to the
hotel. Just then a boy approached us with a telegram. It
was the long awaited message from Miss Mary. She
couldn't get to Quebec that day because it was Sunday and
the trains didn't run, but she'd be there in the morning and
we were not to worry. If the C.P.O. official had seemed like
a knight errant, this certainly was the equivalent of a last
minute reprieve. Now that people were again taking care
of us we stopped feeling like little girls, and we set forth
to the hotel in high spirits, as grand a manner as possible
and one of those quaint vehicles called a calèche. We were
again in proper mental shape to react felicitously to the
picturesque aspects of travel.

The clerk at the Château Frontenac beamed kindly upon
us and gave us a large and comfortable room overlooking
the terrace promenade. The place rather overwhelmed us,
so much so we thought we'd better dress for dinner if not
for anybody in particular. We got into dresses which,
thanks to packing and sea-dampness, looked as if someone
who didn't know how very well had accordion-pleated

them. The maître d'hôtel took one look at us and being
the soul of tact led us to a distant table where, screened by
a pillar and a few discreet palms, we might enjoy the music
and still not distract from the *ton* of his smart clientele.
Once seated we tried to look cool and continental but we
couldn't think of anything to talk about so we sat and
studied the menu. It was in French and this gave me an
opportunity to become offensive and ask Emily if she'd
care to have me translate for her. But she said no, she was
going to order by price anyway. To be sure we were the
guests of the C.P.O. but it seemed hardly grateful for us
to be downing *tournedos de boeuf* at $2.50 when we might
fall to just as heartily on plain *boeuf* at 85¢. I gave the order
in ostentatious French to the waiter who at first appeared
to be deaf but who later turned out to be Greek. A *sommelier* approached us and said "Wine?" and I was deeply
humiliated when Emily answered "Oh, mercy, no!" I
called him back and with a good deal of bravado but not
much acumen ordered a bottle of something that was quite
incorrect for the food we were eating. It was clear that the
sommelier considered it the equivalent of washing down
crêpes suzettes with Moxie. But it was good wine and as
Emily could manage only one glass (wine to her still bore
the flavor of good Indiana brimstone) I drank the rest of
it. After dinner we tried for a time to sit up in a large
formal room, but the strain of the last two days was beginning to tell, and we staggered off to our room. No
matter how tired I am I have an irritating way of becoming
wide awake just before I go to bed, and I wanted to spend
a time talking over everything. Emily flopped instantly
into bed and closed her eyes. The alcoholic content of that
bottle of wine must still have been having its effect for I

remember sitting on the edge of my bed and crying bitterly because I thought Emily wasn't sufficiently interested in our recent peril. She wouldn't sit up and talk about it, she just wanted to go to sleep. Emily pointed out the fact that it was the first sleep she'd had in two nights and I retorted what about me. I not only hadn't slept, she had tramped around on my face. With a muffled "Oh, shut up," Emily sank into oblivion and after crying a little more about our peril I did the same thing.

———————

Early next morning Miss Mary sailed into our room like a rescuing battleship and at the sight of her we shed our sophistication like a pair of shoes that have been pinching for days. All our pent-up emotions of the last 48 hours gave way, and we collapsed onto her turreted bosom and howled because it had all been so awful and we were so glad to see her again, albeit before that moment Emily had never set eyes on her. She later told us we were the dampest pair of adventuresses anyone had ever encountered. Wonderful, overwhelming Miss Mary! She was indeed one of the last of the Titans, in intellect, in physique and in heart. Hers was one of the most stimulating minds of her generation, and with this she had a delicious sense of humor, a zest for life and a warmth of affection that made one instantly adore her. She was over six feet tall and built like a giant oak. Her face was a combination of Martha Washington and the west view of Gibraltar. But at that moment we thought that her great nose, her determined chin and humorous mouth, even her unabashed moustache made up the most wonderful face we had ever seen. We still do. She took immediate charge of us and our luggage and within an

hour we were on the little river boat that plies between
Quebec and Murray Bay. The sun sparkled on the water
and the great Laurentian hills with their toylike villages
moved past on either side and we felt happy and secure. A

group of French Canadian men, very young, sat with their
chairs tilted back against the rail and actually sang "Allouette, gentille allouette, allouette je te plumerai." It was the
first time Emily had ever heard that song and she says she
never hears it now without remembering those handsome
brown heads tilted back in the sun, and their even white
teeth and the fact that she was hearing for the first time a
French song sung not as a foreign language.

It was afternoon when we reached Les Eboulements, the charming little settlement where Miss Mary and her sister Miss Bessie spent their idyllic summers. If Miss Mary was all straight lines from that high granite forehead to the mole on the crag of her chin, Miss Bessie was all comfortable curves and billowing sweetness. Miss Bessie (who never read a book) had accompanied her brilliant sister to French Canada for years but had not bothered to learn a word of French. She and the natives who spoke no English understood one another perfectly. Far more so than in the case of Miss Mary, whose French was of a perfection of idiom and form worthy an academician. But she trumpeted it forth in a good Philadelphia accent which took all nonsense out of the language. It also made her at times quite incomprehensible to the natives, who would look blank and turn for help to Miss Bessie and she, with smiles and gestures, would interpret for her sister.

Their house was an attractive glorified log cabin affair perched on a hill with a magnificent view, half way between the upper and lower villages of the tiny *habitant* settlement of Les Eboulements., It was unspoiled by trippers then and I hope it still is, for the country was incredibly beautiful, the houses quaint and the natives charming. The farmers milked their cows in hillside pastures and then tramped up winding paths beside torrential streams to their snug cottages carrying the milk in copper pails that hung from a wooden yoke across their shoulders. The outside ovens were real and smelt deliciously of good burnt crust, and barefooted children with long poles tended flocks of highly unpleasant but picturesque geese. Emily went pseudo literary and kept saying it was just like Gilbert Parker, which I (who hadn't read Gilbert Parker) thought rather affected of her. But I got even with her by conversing with Miss Mary's local *habitant* domestics in loud and incorrect French.

We were there for a week and it was almost as good as being abroad. We spent the time eating, sleeping, and drinking in Miss Mary's stimulating talk. We read a lot, walked the hills not too strenuously and took one or two shrieking dips into the icy St. Lawrence. One day Miss Mary borrowed her neighbor's Old Dobbin, hitched him to a rural buckboard and took us up a mountain for a picnic. Miss Bessie wore a hat exactly like the one on the horse and Miss Mary rolled her own cigarettes (she could do it with one hand) and talked about Max Beerbohm, Santayana and Walter Pater. We felt very select and rather like "Souls" of the Yellow Book period. On another occasion we had the privilege of going to the "Manoir" for tea. The "Manoir," the Versailles of Les Eboulements, was a sweet old rambling frame house, simply but immaculately maintained in the midst of a formal little box-bordered terrain and owned by the charming and exquisite scion of a vanished age, the local Seigneur (more Gilbert Parker quotes for Emily). He received us with old-fashioned formality and charm, wearing a morning coat and flowered waistcoat. We hadn't thought to wear anything more conventional than our tweed skirts and sweaters and we felt pretty gauche but he treated us graciously, offering us cakes and our choice of poison-strong tea or a domestic cordial made of heaven knows what unless it was a combination of clover, tobacco and laudanum. In spite of our tweed skirts and sweaters and shoes which were only one dollar removed from being sneakers, we found ourselves entering into the formal atmosphere of the "Manoir" and act-

ing as if we were first cousins of the Duc de Guise. I think
the Duc wouldn't have been any too pleased had he seen
me at the unfortunate moment when, after the Seigneur
had asked me to *asseyez-vous* I selected a stiff chair and
moving it to the one spot on that antique floor where one
leg sank into a knot-hole, sat down with a thud and went
over backwards. The Seigneur I've adored ever since, for
he helped right me, apologized for the knot-hole and made
me feel I'd committed no worse misdemeanor than a
sneeze. Miss Mary later enlightened us concerning the status
of this utterly charming individual. "He holds," she said,
"through direct descent his feudal rights by charter from
the king and the people pay him their tithe. While the par-
ish priest rules them morally, the Seigneur looks after their
economic and physical welfare." Little wot we at the time
how his supervision of the latter was going to affect us.

Returning home from the "Manoir" across the fields we
stopped in at a cottage or two where women young and
old, the old ones in white caps, were weaving homespun.
The air inside was stifling. All doors and windows were
closed. That, they explained, was because some of the little
ones had a cold. Some of them even had a slight rash, but
the Seigneur didn't think it was anything. Certainly not
serious enough to warrant calling the district doctor down
from Quebec. We bought a few yards of homespun, chatted with the women and patted the little ones on the head.
It was picturesque as all get out.

On Monday we took the shoreline train back to Quebec.
The weather turned from summer mildness to winter chill.
A fog rolled in, apparently fresh from the Arctic, and lay
like a cold compress over everything. Emily, who thought
that the North Atlantic in June would be about as cool as

Petosky, Michigan, had no garment warmer than that Shakespearean cloak lined with taffeta and Miss Mary marched her off to a stolid Canadian emporium from whence she returned with a stolid Canadian coat. It was easy to see Miss Mary had selected it for her. Emily seemed to have a few misgivings about it herself for as she undid the string of the box she explained, "It's tweed, not too fancy but heavy, and it was only $18.00." What she pulled forth was something that looked like a 19th Century coachman's greatcoat done in black and white check and weighing between fifteen and twenty pounds. It came almost to her ankles and it was embellished with a sort of attached cape, which made it pretty jaunty. There was a chain at the neck for hanging it up. A mere piece of tape wouldn't have held it a moment. It was hard to determine what gave it all that weight, unless possibly rock salt in the hem, for it had very little warmth. When she put it on her knees buckled visibly. But she continued to wear it with the patient fortitude of the peasant woman who is resigned to her heavy load. Later, on shipboard, she acquired a willing gent or two who when they paced the deck with her, would hold it up by the collar to ease off some of the weight so she wouldn't collapse.

The sun came out later in the day and for a time the fog rose and turned into summer clouds. Miss Mary took us to the pier and saw to it that our luggage and selves were safely installed in our stateroom. It was another inside room and again down in what is graphically known as the bowels of the ship, rather in the vicinity of the transverse colon. But the *Empress of France* was a beautiful vessel and even our minimum fare quarters seemed spacious. Miss Mary toured us about the ship, introduced us to the purser and first officer in a manner that implied we had just passed our mid-years at an institute for the feeble-minded, and gave us a lot of advice tó young ladies traveling alone. She particularly stressed the point that nice girls never let themselves be conspicuous. One evening in Les Eboulements, she had read us "Daisy Miller," Henry James' wistful little story about the boy-crazy American girl who gads about Europe in a happy-go-unchaperoned manner which is a blot on the escutcheon of young American womanhood. We must not be Daisy Millers. We must be careful not to create the "wrong impression." A very politic move, she said, would be for us to single out a few nice older women and make friends with them. Politely but without much enthusiasm we told her we would. She kissed us good-bye and went down the gangplank in the manner of a dreadnought being launched. On the dock she turned and waved and then shouted in her wonderful Main Line accent: "Don't forget, girls, get close to some nice women!" which shamed us as profoundly as it fascinated all nearby passengers who eyed us as if we might prove to be a light fingered team and Miss Mary our boss who was giving us some last minute instructions in code.

CHAPTER 3

THEY treated us royally on the *Empress of France*. This was due partly to a certain pull Miss Mary had with the line and partly to the fact that we were survivors of the ill-fated *Montcalm*. We were allotted places at the First Officer's table, our deck chairs were admirably situated and no sooner had the ship got under way than a diminutive cabin-boy knocked at our door and presented the captain's compliments and an invitation to come to his quarters that afternoon for tea. And maybe that didn't make us fluttery! We fixed ourselves up to look as much as we could like the sweethearts of the crew and on the stroke of four-thirty went where I called "aloft" and Emily, who said I was just showing off, called "upstairs." Not realizing there might be an inner companionway, we climbed the outside ladder on the windy side. I grabbed my skirt in time to wedge it elegantly between my knees but Emily arrived with hers well over her head like an inside-out umbrella from which she emerged quite flustered and saying "Oh, mercy me!" Despite Henry James and that broken engagement, Emily in times of confusion went definitely Indiana. The Commander, Captain Griffiths, was a darling, very hearty, very old sea-dog. His eyes were of that quality of blue that seems to come only from a lifetime of staring out on limitless water, and his cheeks, with an autumnal tracery of little red veins, looked as if they had buffeted years of gales. He gave us tea, delicious slices of thin bread and butter and some generous hunks of that forthright British cake which, one feels, in a case of necessity could serve as a mooring. We devoured everything with delight, all the time saying we really couldn't and the captain who knew better insisting that we could. Happy, happy girlhood! Hip-free and not yet calory-conscious, we'd have downed a suckling pig if he'd had it handy. Emily, that child of inland plains, was somewhat dumbfounded by her nautical surroundings. I found myself doing most of the talking. I don't know why people when they converse with sea captains feel they must stick exclusively to the subject of ships and sea-faring, but they do and I was no exception. I went heartily yo-heave-ho and talked in a tone that implied we were in a heavy blow, until Emily hissed at me, "The man isn't deaf." He was very forbearing, was Captain Griffiths. He listened politely while I told him how many times I'd crossed and when I said how much I loved the sea he smiled indulgently. Fired by my own enthusiasm I went on to say that my ancestors had been Nantucket whalers, which was even a surprise to myself. No ancestor of mine ever saw Nantucket, much less a whale. But it seemed a colorful idea at the time.

Tea finished, Captain Griffiths took us into the wheelhouse and we each had a turn at steering the ship, that is, we each held on to a spoke like the little girl in "The Helping Hand" while the quartermaster turned the wheel. We gawped at a lot of instruments we didn't understand and when they were explained to us said "Oh, I see," but we didn't. At one point, Emily, by way of conversation, asked, "Will there be any icebergs, do you think?" and the captain with a cheery smile said "Yes, lots" as if he were referring to Eskimo Pies at a picnic. Then he took us into the chart room where he showed us our course, which lay sweet as could be right through the thick of the ice district. Ours was the first ship of the season to venture through the treacherous Straits of Belle Isle, he said, and that was fun too. As if that hadn't succeeded in bringing our hearts into our gullets, he showed us a sheaf of wireless despatches from the U.S. Ice Patrol. Each reported the latitude and longitude of a berg and ended with the ominous words "Good luck." Emily's eyes protruded like those of a startled Pekingese and in an attempt to soothe her I said, "Then it's all right. They know just where the bergs are," to which the captain said happily, "Yes, but ice can shift in a very few minutes and in a fog there's no way of telling."

At that precise moment there came a sudden and terrifying blast of sound that shattered our ears and nerves. The foghorn was directly over our heads and with the vibration of its roaring voice the whole vessel seemed to shudder. Certainly we did. The captain dropped the chart he was holding and looked up. Our eyes followed him to the window. It was one of those uncompromising windows which went all the way around so you couldn't possibly miss anything you'd like to. At the moment it appeared to have been suddenly packed on the outer side with cotton. That fog we'd sampled in Quebec had returned and appeared to have settled for the summer. It had completely blotted out the nearby shoreline and it lay in thick drifts on the water. Even the mainmast and rigging were blurred and like those of some phantom ship. The captain assumed one of those "rounding the Horn" expressions and we said that maybe we'd better be going back to our cabins although, as we went below, Emily said that where she'd rather be going back to was Buffalo. She was frankly scared and that was the only reason I wasn't. The rare times I ever approach having even a semblance of courage is when I'm with someone more frightened than I usually am. At this point I was brave as a lion. Every time the foghorn blew I'd jump but then look heroic and say wasn't it a thrilling sound and as long as there was nobody more nautically informed to hear me, I became quite technical. To reassure her I described certain mechanical devices they had for sounding and for detecting ice, as if I'd recognize a mechanical device if I fell over it, which is what I'd have been most apt to do. Most of this information, as in the case of those whaling ancestors of mine, was purely fictitious but it pacified her somewhat and we changed into dinner clothes, which made us feel rather gallant. And then the foghorn blew less frequently and finally stopped altogether. That made us feel very brave indeed. The fog had let up and that load being lifted from our minds we decided it was about time we started in following Miss Mary's advice about meeting some nice women. We went upstairs and found that the majority of the ship's company had collected in the bar for cocktails. We would have liked a cocktail but were restrained by the fear of making that "wrong impression," and also by not knowing what to ask for. So we ordered, only because we'd heard someone say it was a lady's drink, a couple of Porto-flips, a nasty concoction all eggs, sweet port and gunk like the stuff they gave me after typhoid to build me up. And that created an impression, on us, at any rate. We killed the taste to a certain degree by smoking cigarettes (which was also pretty daring of us). We had only recently gained parental permission to smoke and we did it in the manner of novices, puffing like mad, because we thought if one didn't, the light would go out. We cast a few polite glances at such women as Miss Mary might consider nice, but received no encouragement. We also, when we thought the other wasn't looking, sneaked a few surreptitious looks at such men as *we* might consider nice. There didn't appear to be any spare ones. A man in his thirties to us was middle-aged.

Our outlook brightened at dinner when we found ourselves next to two young doctors. Their names were Paul White and Joseph Aub and they are now among Boston's most distinguished physicians, but at that time were freshly hatched out of medical school. They were just enough our seniors to make us, accustomed as we were to Yale and even Lawrenceville contemporaries, place them in that glamorous category of "older men." After dinner they asked us to join them for coffee and liqueurs and that certainly set us up. The previous year in Paris I had once or twice had a giddy thimbleful of Anisette so I ordered that while Emily without batting an eyelid called for a crème de menthe. She later admitted it was the only liqueur she knew about. Her mother used to give her a coffee-spoonful of it after a dose of castor oil to take the taste away. An orchestra played in the hall outside and we felt continental as could be. I remember thinking young Dr. Aub must be very much a man of the world because he spoke of having once taken Eva Le Gallienne out to lunch. The evening passed pleasantly and we retired at an early hour still having met no women. But, we said, could we help it if men were attracted to us first? And we smiled in modest apology.

"I guess," Emily murmured as she dozed off to sleep, and

it would seem the crème de menthe had had its effect, "we're just another case of the Daisy Miller of the present diller."

_____

Emily is the type who never lets on if she doesn't understand. Refusing ever to ask about things, she believes in making stabs on her own. If you try to explain or show her she gets mad. The first morning out, the bath-steward announced that her bath was ready and she swept out after him trailing towel and dropping oddments of soap and talcum powder as if it were all an old and somewhat boring story to her. On her return she complained that the bath had put her neck out of joint.

"How could a bath put your neck out of joint?"

"Sniffing."

"Sniffing what?"

"The fresh water."

"Sniffing what fresh water? What in heaven's name are you talking about?"

It appears that when she entered the bath, she was confronted by a tub filled with hot water and that seemed reasonable enough. Across it, however, was a board and on that a basin also filled with water and that struck her as being very odd. The steward enquired if Modom's bath was as Modom liked it and Modom said brightly that it was just fine, shut and bolted the door, threw off her raiment and launched herself into the tub. The temperature of the water was perfect and except for the fact that the soap had suddenly lost its ability to lather, it was all that one might desire in the way of a bath. She was more than ever mystified by the presence of that extra basin. Then, with the sudden inspiration of a Sherlock Holmes she figured out what it was for. She had once heard my mother say that the only thing that ever made her sea-sick was the smell of hot salt water in the morning. "Of course!" she said. "This is to ward off possible mal-de-mer. You sit in the tub and keep sniffing the more rarefied air above the basin of hot water." Emily is not a tall girl and even if she had been, she'd have required some giraffe blood to have enabled her to span the distance. But she tried valiantly until she felt she was becoming like Alice after she'd swallowed the "Eat me" tablet. She was quite put out and so was her neck, and when amid yells of derision I explained that the basin was for soaping and the tub for rinsing, she became even more so.

We spent the morning on deck. The weather was sparkling and the fog of the previous afternoon was like something we'd imagined. To be sure there was a bank of slate-colored cloud on the eastern horizon but that didn't bother us. We felt full of health and that sense of well-being that is classified as animal spirits. Emily for the time forgot her antipathy to sea-faring and leaned on the rail gazing romantically at the water and quoting Homer in the original, which I considered (and still do) extremely elaborate of her. Her stock quotation, a phrase which translated meant "the wine-dark sea," she kept addressing to the St. Lawrence which at that point was azure blue and didn't in the least resemble wine. And who was she, a daughter of Indiana, to know about wine, anyway?

That day we again looked about for those nice women but without much enthusiasm and without any results. The married women were pre-occupied with their husbands and children and outside some dismal creatures who were banded together in "Miss Somebody's Tour," the only un-

attached females were two extremely hearty English girls
with bright pink hands and a vocabulary which seldom ex-
ceeded the bounds of "I say" and "Right-o." We dismissed
them as a couple of Girl Guides in mufti. But toward the
afternoon of the following day they approached us with
exuberant spirits and a formal-looking piece of paper and
asked us would we care to enter the tournament. They
assured us it was going to be "frightfully ripping" (or
maybe it was "jolly deese") and that Sir Michael Nairn
was going to be referee. Obligingly we put down our
names with the happy innocence of the average woman
who signs a proxy without the slightest knowledge of what
it means. For all we knew about the tournament it might
be anything from bridge to the sort the Black Prince was
so handy at. We were young enough still to harbor the glad
illusion that organized forms of get-together were commendable. But it was less a prompting of community spirit
that decided us to sign up, than that mention of Sir Michael
Nairn who had been pointed out to us as the distinguished
note on the passenger list. Traveling with him were his
wife and daughter. If Sir Michael were going to keep score,
we'd surely feel we were on speaking terms with him and
then in no time at all we'd get introduced to Lady Nairn
and that daughter who despite the fact that she seemed
slightly aloof and as if when she was born they'd found
"The Honorable" in distinguished strawberry marks under
her left shoulder, looked to be about our own age and very
attractive. Here was our golden opportunity for meeting
those nice women. Nobility to boot. Miss Mary would indeed be proud of us. As we eagerly scribbled our signatures
one of the Girl Guides said it ought to be heaps of fun,
simply heaps and we echoed yes, heaps. Then she said she

for one was frightfully keen on tournaments and we said so were we and as soon as she'd cantered away we set about finding out what the heck sort of tournament we'd gotten ourselves in for. It proved to be deck-tennis and that was one prospect that didn't please. For all my much vaunted ocean crossings, I had never played deck-tennis. Neither had Emily. For that matter, with the exception of our brief sojourn on the *Montcalm*, she had never been on a deck. What vague misgivings we had, we subdued with the optimistic belief that our numbers would not come up until the tournament was well under way and in the interim we could practice up. We might even get out early of a morning and do some special cramming. The athletic aspects of the affair were of minor importance in comparison with our getting cosy with those nice and noble women.

I think this is the proper moment to state that Emily and I are not of the breed of amazons. We're no good at sports and we weren't then. At Bryn Mawr I played hockey only because it was compulsory. My team was the seventh, which seldom met, owing to the fact that there was no other team inadequate enough to meet us. I tried basketball (also compulsory) but if anyone had the lack of judgment to toss a ball at me I ducked it and ran. The only outstanding feat I ever accomplished in that repulsively degrading activity known familiarly as "gym," was to knock myself senseless with an Indian club. Emily wasn't one whit better, if truth were told. But in her case truth wasn't told and the thought riles me to this day. She was small and moved gracefully (I was tall and moved like a McCormick reaper). Moreover, she had side-stepped all regulation college athletics by having talked somebody into allowing her to be an instructor in an activity she chose to call "rhythmic dancing." I don't believe she had the remotest notion of what she was doing, let alone teaching, but she had picked up an Isadora Duncan outfit and a few Attic postures and when she told the head of the athletic department she had a special contribution to give the students, the

head of the athletic department, whose only contribution wasn't much more than a hockey-stick and an old pair of sneakers, let her get away with it. I am not one to write with authority about Emily's class in Greek whatever-it-was. I attended it only once. Emily on this occasion wore a lovely little purple tunic, very bacchanalian, very ballet russe. The only reason she wasn't carrying a bunch of grapes in her teeth was because the grape season was over. The rest of us bacchantes had perforce to wear our regulation athletic attire, middy-blouse, serge bloomers, woollen stockings and some tasty black foot-gear known as "gym shoes," which looked as if they'd been cut down out of arctics. Emily, who by comparison had no trouble at all looking like Pavlowa, had us all prancing, expressing joy, sorrow, frolic and greeting, the while a grim individual at an upright accompanied us with "Narcissus" and "Nights of Gladness." Despite my middy-blouse and serge bloomers I tried my most passionately to act like something hot off Keats' Grecian urn, but Emily said I was a disrupting element in the class and put me out. To avoid further exertion I got myself relegated to a defective posture and spinal curvature list, a select group who were on their honor to do corrective exercises in their rooms. Emily, meanwhile, by conducting her class of bloomered hamadryads, got out of hockey and such, which perhaps was a lucky break for all concerned. Our sportive prowess beyond the bourne of college was no less brilliant. I had ridden a mule down the Grand Canyon and could swim in tepid, calm water. Emily could play a fair game of croquet and had climbed Mt. Tamalpais. Heaven knows what made us think we could now play deck-tennis, unless it was that goading thought of getting close to Scottish nobility. How close, we had yet to learn.

Next morning we arrived in the dining-room at our usual breakfast hour, which was just as the doors were about to close. The Girl Guides were leaving at their customary single-foot. In passing our table one of them reined herself in and neighed into Emily's startled ear: "I say! You've drawn first play!"

"First play?" Emily croaked.

"Lucky you!" she whinnied in envy. "Your match comes up immediately after breck," and she loped away.

Emily looked slightly ill. "My match may not be the

only thing that's coming up," she said. She wasn't dressed for deck-tennis, not that either of us had brought along any deck-tennis outfits. But that particular morning she was wearing high heels, a blue silk skirt and a frilly blouse which stayed tucked in at the waist only if she kept her arms down. We gulped our coffee and started for the cabin to ferret out garments that would be more *pour le sport.* On the stairs we were overtaken by the Girl Guides who appeared to be in a state of frenzy. The first match had been scheduled to start fifteen minutes ago and they were all waiting for Emily. She mumbled something about getting into proper clothes but they said nonsense, she'd be all right. However, she must really get on with it because after all they meant to say as it were, one couldn't keep Sir Michael waiting, now, could one? And between them they hustled her off and onto the top deck where an alarmingly large group had assembled to witness the opening match.

I followed after with a sinking heart. I am one who suffers acute stage fright for my friends and on this occasion I had reason. Joe Aub and Paul White had found a place to watch from a portion of the top deck which overlooked the court. I took a stand beside them and near a lifeboat so that I could jump in it and hide if I found I couldn't bear to look. Ours was an all too uninterrupted view of the goings on. The much-heralded scorekeeper, Sir Michael Nairn, was directly below us where we could spit on him if the impulse became irresistible. Emily, wearing her high heels and a grin which might easily have betokened imbecility but which I knew only too well was the mask for a blue funk, was standing with three men of the realm. They were impeccably clad in white flannels, blazers that had coats of arms on the pockets, and those swankly casual mufflers one knows may any minute be ripped off to reveal a desperately manly throat. The good luck of which the Girl Guide was so envious had continued even beyond drawing the opening match. She had further drawn three unknown men to make up the two pairs of players (doubles it was) and not a woman, not even one of those nice ones. Joe and Paul knew all about it. Emily, they said, had landed as partner an Australian champion who held the all-high in deck-tennis the world around. Emily was talking with him now. Judging by the snatches of conversation which floated up to us, we gathered she was asking how the game was played. The Australian champion blanched for a moment, then relaxed into an indulgent burst of laughter and said, "That's a good one." It was clear he thought she was just having her little joke. Emily laughed, too, but not so heartily. Someone handed her a rope ring and she looked at it as if uncertain whether she was expected to wear it or balance it on her nose. She caught sight of me and for a moment her expression was that of someone who has just been asked to say grace at Buckingham Palace; but with admirable control she smiled and waved the quoit which she then immediately dropped and her partner, shocked as if she had dropped the flag, retrieved it for her. Sir Michael blew a sort of traffic whistle and the four players stepped out onto the court. I was fascinated to see Emily making in the general direction of Sir Michael Nairn the sort of little formal bow trapeze artists execute before taking off their cloaks. The Australian champion drew first serve and relieving Emily of the quoit left her foot-loose and fancy-free while he did the work. All she had to do was watch and learn and occasionally change courts. The game was a walk-over for them. Sir Michael called out an impressive "Forty-Love" and smiled approvingly.

The second game was all right too. A gentleman of the opposing team did the serving and on her side of the net Emily's partner did all the catching and they also won that game. Emily's partner must have been wondering why she didn't exert herself more, for occasionally as an easy toss came her way he'd call out, "Yours!" But Emily with an "I wouldn't dream of depriving you of it" smile would shake her head and let the ring pass and the long Australian arm would reach out and catch it in the nick of time. Then came Emily's turn and I began getting ready to crawl off into the lifeboat. Her partner handed her the ring and she took it with a brave flourish. Emily is a born mimic and her manner of tossing was a faithful replica of his, but the result wasn't the same. She must have given it an extra fillip or held her thumb in it after she flung it. Or maybe it had something to do with the champion's hailing from Australia. Whatever the cause, the ring, the moment it left her hand turned into a little boomerang. It would start out across the net, hesitate in mid-air, then curve on around and miraculously land back at Emily's feet. Every time she served, it would describe that astonishing parabola and like a homing pigeon return whence it started unless it encountered some obstacle in passage, and the only object it ever encountered was the face of Sir Michael Nairn. The impact in most instances stopped the pretty plaything in its flight, but occasionally it would just graze the bridge of that Raeburn-esque nose and then come winging back to mama. The object scored a number of direct hits before Sir Michael, whose astonishment must have slowed up his reflexes, retired behind a stanchion. There he was comparatively safe but he couldn't keep what, for lack of a better name, they called the score unless like good King Wenceslaus he occasionally looked out and every time he did Little

Australia was whizzing by and he got it right and proper. People watched with gaping immobility. One or two giggled nervously. I wanted to go hide but the spectacle held me spellbound. Emily's face had taken on that fresh bortsch

hue. She emitted occasional little squeals and at one time came out with the astonishing remark, "Dear me! There's such a strong wind!" which made the other players think her demented. It was one of those days of breathless calm when the smoke rises from the stacks in perpendicular columns. Finally into Emily's desperate eye there came a glint of determination. With the pent-up frenzy of despair she aimed and instead of twirling the ring, threw it like a baseball. This time there was no boomerang action. Swift as an arrow that rope doughnut shot at a tangent from the court, over the heads of the rapturous audience, down to the second-class promenade and spun the cap off an officer who was just coming out on deck. Cap and missile went overboard and the officer turned right around and went back inside. That formed a sort of climax. The match was declared null or void or something and the three men shook hands but I don't remember anyone shaking hands with Emily. Joe, Paul and I were recovering behind a funnel when Emily joined us. We decided we'd better not try to approach Sir Michael just yet . . . maybe after the swelling had gone down. It would be just as well to avoid the Australian champion too and remain inconspicuous for a while.

We never met up with Lady Nairn and her aristocratic daughter or any other nice women. As a matter of fact, we never met up with any women at all. Instead we went around with a male assortment which ranged from our two nice doctors to a Princeton lad who throughout the entire voyage remained conscientiously intoxicated. There was also a merchant from Brussels whose English was not his strong point and whose constant leit motif was "I no understand, you see I am Belch," and an English lecturer on New Thought or some such thing with whom I was quite impressed because I thought he had such stimulating ideas. I remember one statement by which I was particularly moved, "England and the United States must get together." We were, in our simple fashion, having a whirl and it was without much reluctance that we forwent the companionship of women and resigned ourselves to being Messalinas.

———————

For the first two or three days we had been within sight of the ever-widening shores of the St. Lawrence. We were now reaching the treacherous Straits of Belle Isle. Fog, the quality of damp, chill lamb's wool, rolled in to smother the land, the sea and the ship. The foghorn started its mournful reiterant barking and kept it up at two minute intervals for three mortal days and nights. Everyone became jittery. The captain later told us that from a fog and ice point of view, it was the worst crossing he'd ever known. Emily and I were frankly terrified, only I harbored the misguided idea that it wasn't cricket to admit to being scared stiff so I hid as best I could my state of scare and just stayed stiff. Emily, on the other hand, in giving vent to her terror was better off. She'd endure the rasp of the foghorn just so long, then rush to the cabin and lie prostrate on her berth with pillows piled on top of her head to shut out the sound. Then it would occur to her that maybe the boat was sinking and no one had remembered her, so she'd gallop up onto the deck in the general vicinity of our emergency station to see if anyone wanted her. I recall one especially dismal morning when the air was bitterly cold and the fog so dense you quite literally couldn't see your hand in front of your face (that is if you had any particular reason for wanting to see your hand in front of your face). The *Empress*, her engines slowed up to a point of making her quiver as if in apprehension, was creeping along at just enough speed to keep to the course. Seamen kept lowering strange objects for taking the temperature of the water and when they studied the results, their expression was that of a nurse who reads a thermometer and tells you your temperature is 99° when she knows it's 104°. Chunks of field ice occasionally scraped the sides of the ship. Shadows in the fog rift took on fantastic shapes and most terrifying of all, one could plainly hear an answering repetition of the bark of our horn, an echo reverberating from a nearby iceberg. The ice was here, the ice was there, the ice was all around, and I for one was on the lookout for an albatross. Suddenly from somewhere out in that cold, drifting nightmare, came the thin wail of a conch shell. A fishing smack was almost under our bow and we were about to run her down. Her piteous cry was answered by a series of quick blasts from our siren, signaling instructions to avoid a collision, and the tiny vessel passed safely by to starboard. This occurred during one of those intervals when Emily was doing her ostrich act. I who was watching the incident by the rail turned to someone and said, "I bet that'll bring Emily up on deck." Before I had pronounced the word "deck" a door burst open and through it shot Emily, goggle-eyed, disheveled and carrying two life-jackets. For an effective moment or two she stood on the threshold looking doomed but gallant, then seeing the rest of us as yet weren't taking to the boats, she dropped the jackets behind a door, stepped forth with elaborate unconcern, lit a shaky cigarette and announced she'd just come out for a stroll. Although it was arctic weather, she had left off the tweed coat (I think she was afraid that once wet it would drag her down under) but what she hadn't left off was a pair of blush-pink satin mules.

Fog wasn't the only hazard of sea-faring that got Emily down. She was never able to accustom herself to the ship's noises. Our cabin being low in price, the location was near the baggage-room. I have never been able to fathom just what goes on in a baggage-room. At specified periods throughout the entire crossing there will issue from it intermittent series of thudding, banging and dropping sounds, all rather violent and accompanied by sudden bursts of animated and seemingly threatening voices shouting in what would appear to be a completely unknown tongue. The impression is that all movable luggage is being ruthlessly scattered about by a surprise boarding-party who speak only Esperanto. Emily never became accustomed to it. Whenever those curious sounds broke loose—particularly in the middle of the night—she'd sit up in bed, switch on the light and cry accusingly, "You see? Mutiny!" Another thing which perturbed her was the early morning hosing of the decks. Even way down in our little grey home on the keel, we could hear streams of water swishing busily several decks above us. Emily never heard it without calling out the startling announcement "We're awash!"

The fog, like the snow in Hiawatha, grew ever thicker, thicker, thicker. Field ice continued crunching against the sides of the ship and those echoes of the foghorn from nearby bergs became more frequent. Even the crew was tense. One evening at dinner the orchestra chose as a selection for the soup course the overture from "William Tell" beginning it with a nasty clash of cymbals, followed by an

ominous rolling of drums. Every officer in the dining-room
jumped to his feet and one or two started for his post be-
lieving we really had rammed an iceberg. When the startling opening turned into the familiar strains of the "Dance
des Vaches" they sat down sheepishly. There was a lot of
artificial laughter and everyone tried to pass it off as a
joke. But we didn't feel particularly jocular. That night
nobody danced and nobody went to bed. People sat in
the main lounge distractedly playing cards or reading copies
of *Punch* upside down. Some walked the deck as if it were
the floor of the death house cell. A few intelligent ones
stayed in the bar and deliberately ossified themselves. We
were still too naïve to realize the wisdom of this last expe-
dient, so we sat shivering in our deck chairs saying nothing
and hoping we'd be able to meet the end in the grand manner of the gentlewomen we'd been told to be. Along toward
two in the morning an officer ashen from lack of sleep
descended from the bridge. He went from group to group
saying something—what it was we dreaded to hear. Finally
he reached our end of the deck when he gave out the
heavenly information: "The captain's compliments and he
would like the passengers to know that we are now clear
of the iceberg zone and that the fog is lifting." And then
gradually, miraculously the damp lamb's wool became less
and less dense and began taking on a strange luminous
quality like some sort of celestial Christmas tree trimming.
This, in turn, tore apart and dissolved and there was a
large comfortable moon and a sea ruffled only by the little
ripples running in and out of the great path of lunar reflection which raced along beside us as the engines began to
pick up tempo. The weather had lifted, the skies were
clear, and one was again aware of the power and the glory
of going FULL SPEED AHEAD.

CHAPTER 4

THE next evening, two days before we were to land, was the night of the ship's concert. I had been asked to participate and had agreed with alacrity. Those were the happy days when with that confidence of a Bernhardt which is vouchsafed only to the amateur I would recite at the drop of a hat and if nobody dropped a hat I'd recite anyway. My repertoire included Noyes's "Highwayman," a few gems in Italian and Negro dialect and (I shudder to recall) Lady Macbeth's sleepwalking scene. I spent an afternoon going over some of my choicer selections in the seclusion of our cabin, and partly because I thought it was professional, but more in order to annoy Emily, went about muttering "Mi-mi-mi" and other embarrassing vocalizations. The morning of the concert dawned, and I woke to the realization that my enthusiasm had lost some of its brightness. My throat was scrapy, my nose stopped up and it was all too apparent that I was giving birth to a fine young cold. I blamed it on the fog of the past three days and tried curing myself by lying in the sun on the top deck, where a series of vicious drafts played on my most vulnerable parts, and the smokestacks showered upon me a gentle rain of soot. By mid-afternoon my throat felt like something dangling from a hook in a butcher's shop. Someone advised me to gargle salt and water, and Emily, who went on the theory that if one pill is good for you, five are even better, mixed up a concoc-

tion so thick with salt it strangled me into near uncon-
sciousness. Somebody gave me some aspirin and somebody
else gave me pyramidon and somebody else gave me something else and I swallowed it all quite indiscriminately,
muttering brave remarks to the effect that "The show
must go on." Toward evening I began to feel better, if
slightly light-headed. I gulped down a cup of soup, dressed
and put on a semblance of a make-up. That was one of the
features of my dramatic display in those days. Whenever
I recited, even if in a small living-room, I went on the
theory that a full theatrical make-up was requisite. On this
occasion I noticed that my eyes were somewhat glazed
and that my cheeks didn't need much rouge, but I at-
tributed this to excitement. The hour for the concert was
announced by a boy banging a gong, and I went to the
main saloon. My act wasn't due till toward the end of
the program, and for the first half I sat at one side behind
the temporary stage. It was one of those routine ship's
concerts. There was the usual little man who told endless
stories in Lancashire dialect beginning with "I'm minded
of the man who . . ." which nobody understood, but over
which everybody roared politely; and that lady with the
soprano voice and bust who sang all about "When I was a
young lad before my beard was gray," to whom everyone
listened with fitting expressions of gloom. The orchestra
played those selections from Victor Herbert they'd been
giving every night, and a sailor with a talent for the trom-
bone obliged with an ear-splitting rendition of "Rocked in
the Cradle of the Deep." I listened in a daze, alternately
burning with heat and shivering with chill. There was a
high sea outside and the boat was doing a lot of pitching
and tossing, which made things slightly awkward, as the

temporary platform, which was on sort of casters, would roll with the motion until it was stopped on either end by a pillar, in an abrupt contact which would hurtle it back the other way. The performers had to take a wide stance and hold onto any handy bit of furniture for support. My turn was drawing near, and Emily and I both began growing pretty nervous. Just before I went on, that conscientious drinker from Princeton brought me a hooker of straight brandy and that did the trick. It also made me sway, but in a rhythm that was in counterpose to that of the ship, so I remained fairly steady. I have absolutely no memory of what I did, but it was apparently a hit. In fact mine was a "success" that could really be called *fou*. This must have been due to the fact that the preceding acts had been so terrible mine must have looked pretty good in contrast. Also the brandy and that mixture of medicine had freed me of all inhibitions and I acted with a fine abandon. There was considerable applause and I was in a flush of what I mistook for success. The concert was followed by a gala dance with confetti and favors and those paper hats middle-aged people, if they're drunk, think are funny. The dance floor was crowded and we were never off it. I knew by now that I was ill but I didn't care. Mine was the "tomorrow we die" spirit. I felt like the Dame aux Camellias and as if a breath would blow me away. With my hectic flush I didn't look much like the Dame aux Camellias and the only breath blowing was my brandy-laden own. I danced madly with everybody. It is like a kaleidoscopic delirium to me now but I can dimly remember the orchestra playing the "Blue Danube" and my whirling in a dizzy waltz with Joe Aub and thinking I was pretty *Alt Wien.* I also have a distinct recollection of going out on

deck with that Pride of Princeton and letting him kiss me.
Girls didn't kiss much in those days. Those who did were
considered "fast." We still had ringing in our consciences
the maternal admonition that "boys would lose all respect
for us if we did." Whenever I fell from grace in this fash-

ion (which was whenever I had the slightest opportunity)
I'd go through an aftermath of abject penitence, accusing
myself of being a Magdalen . . . without having a very
clear idea of what a Magdalen was, then when the occasion next offered itself I'd do it all over again. That night
my abandon was so complete I felt no remorse. As a matter of fact I was incapable of feeling anything beyond a
sore throat and a perpetual dry heat-wave.

I have no memory of ever getting to bed but I certainly

remember waking up in the early morning and thinking I
had a combination of pneumonia and diphtheria with a
slight sprinkling of small-pox. I was much too ill to move.
My breathing came with effort and a sound like a thresh-
ing machine. I moaned and lay staring at the ceiling waiting for the Fatal Reaper. Emily woke and looked at me
and it was clear she was scared. She dressed and went
forth to summon the ship's physician, then prompted by
some fortuitous inner hunch, decided it might be wiser to
get hold of one of our doctor friends. She found Joe Aub
and in a frenzy yanked him down to the cabin. He looked
me over, listened to my lungs and punched my stomach
which, with the memory of our recent "Blue Danube"
whirl bright within me, at once embarrassed and rather
pleased me. Then he told me to say "Ah" and after I had he
looked extremely grave.

"Have you ever had measles?" he asked.

"Measles? Why, no."

"Well, my dear girl," he said, "you're coming down
with a hell of a case."

"Measles!" I couldn't believe him. "But I thought I was
past the age for such things."

"Adults can have measles," he said. "And when they do
it's pretty serious."

"But how on earth . . ." Then I remembered Les
Eboulements. Those picturesque little French Canadian in-
teriors, the windows and doors hermetically closed, and
the little children running about underfoot, some with a
rash, others flushed, and all of them coughing generously
in every direction.

Paul White came down and verified Joe's diagnosis, and
then came the problem of what to do. Nobody must know

about it. The boat was due at Cherbourg early next morning and a few hours later Emily and I were to disembark at Southampton. If it became known I had measles they'd never let me land. The ship, after a day or two in Southampton, was to go on to Hamburg and I'd be sent in all probability to a German quarantine hospital. The prospect was too awful. I lay back on the pillows and amid a torrent of tears wailed that I didn't want to go to Germany and be nursed by a walkyrie. They pacified me as best they could. Paul and Joe promised to give me all medical attention, even if of a clandestine nature, and Emily could nurse me. She had had measles (and that was one more thing that made me feel inferior, like her spouting Greek or her annoying ability to quote William James). I'd be all right for twenty-four hours, as the rash wouldn't come out for a time, and somehow they'd manage to devise some way to smuggle me into England. (One might have thought I was a pearl necklace or a shipment of narcotics.)

The three of them went up on deck and into a huddle behind a lifeboat, where they made a solemn agreement. Emily would not report my contagious condition to the ship's doctor and neither would Paul or Joe. They might be disbarred or unfrocked or whatever it is that happens to medical men, but they'd throw in their lot with ours and take the risk. My parents were planning to be at Southampton. We'd had a wire saying so. Once having safely run the gamut of the health inspector I could go direct to a hotel where Mother would take care of me. Joe had to get off at Cherbourg but Paul would go on through to England with us and see me started on my way to recovery. Mother would in due course write the captain that what we'd thought was a cold had turned into measles, so they could fumigate the cabin and prevent any further spread of the disease,—as if, the preceding evening, I hadn't already spread it in a manner capable of starting an all-high European epidemic. The main hope was that my rash wouldn't manifest itself until they'd gotten me safely on land. They returned to tell me all this, but I was too sick to care. The two doctors managed to get just enough of the proper medicine from the ship's infirmary without exciting too much suspicion, and I spent the forenoon in a stupor, roused now and then by Emily, who would shine a painfully bright miniature flash-light (I believe they were called "bug-lights") in my face, study its condition and say in the tone of someone trying to pep up a losing team: "You hold that rash back!"

Later I was left comparatively alone. The day was balmy, there was a smell of land in the air and after those hours of dank fog and slate-colored sky Emily was much too elated to bother about my measles. The misty outline of a headland lay like a cloud bank on the northern horizon. Gulls flew out to form a circling, soaring convoy, their cries like the creak of a pulley, the late afternoon sun gilding their fat snowy bellies. Fishing boats suddenly appeared and small craft began dotting the sea, making it seem a friendly lake. Occasionally someone would call out from the calm water below in a voice that rang with the unmistakable lilt of Ireland. Night came on, and over the port bow the great warning of the Fastness light began flashing. Emily watched it all with wonder and a few tears, and then came down to our little pest-hole to see if I were still alive and to do some packing. She moved me into the upper berth because she said it was airier and I'd be more comfortable up there, but I suspect her real motive was to get me out of the way. Then she proceeded to pack in the manner of an excited nineteen-year-old girl, which is the same manner as that of someone salvaging odds and ends from a burning house. We'd struck a ground swell and the ship was rolling slowly but decidedly. Things Emily was in the act of packing slid alternately under the berth and the couch. Bottles fell over and tooth brushes clattered about in the basin. Emily cursed and I groaned. Every now and then she'd make me down a pill or a spoonful of medicine. At other times she'd hand me a glass of something to gargle, then holding up a homely object known in some locales as a "thunder-mug" she'd say in the dulcet tone of a night nurse, "Come on, dear, spit for Emily." It was a ghastly night. I was really awfully sick and Emily was really awfully scared. I tossed and moaned and Emily in helpless despair kept getting up and putting cool cloths on my brow and making me spit for Emily. Neither of us slept until toward dawn when from sheer exhaustion we dozed off and immediately afterward our slumber was shattered by those early morning noises which all steamship personnel consider a necessary accompaniment to coming into harbor. Baggage is hurtled and banged along passageways, people scamper quite a lot, and a sleepy cabin-boy whangs a gong for some special reveille-hour breakfast which nobody dreams of going to.

We were coming into Cherbourg and Emily went up on deck to look at it and to indulge in another spell of emotional appreciation. One's view of France after a long absence, no matter how well one knows it, is something to bring a slight lump into the throat. But to the girl of nineteen, seeing it for the first time, it was a thing to produce a lump the size of a healthy orange. A hazy poilu-blue sky, flecked with those harmless little clouds that seem to form only over France; a smooth grey sea, gashed by a long breakwater the color of a dark wet seal. Along the breakwater a handful of men in faded blue pants, red handkerchiefs tied loosely about their throats, sat fishing the way Frenchmen from time immemorial have fished, which is with a long pole, the air of a *philosophe* and no thought of ever catching a fish. In the misty distance lay the sweet French coast, the ancient town, like a model for a stage set, and the jetty with its custom-house striped like peppermint candy to indicate you were approaching a country where people were gay and, just in case you weren't certain it was France, on a nearby building, a huge painted likeness of that dreadful leering baby, the Savon Cadum ad.

The ship had dropped anchor and a small French tender had pulled up alongside and taken off such passengers as were destined for Cherbourg. They were about to push off, and there was that usual *crise de nerfs* which seems to accompany all French maritime manoeuvres. Whistles blew shrilly, sailors with red pompons either rushed about gesticulating madly or stood quite still with elaborate indifference and shrugged while people in the pilot house engaged themselves in vituperative argument, and frazzled Americans ambled hopelessly about looking for bits of missing luggage. Seething with activity, the tender started for shore, and the *Empress*, with a short snort of relief from her horn, began hauling in her anchor. A few yards away there burst from the tender a series of whistle tootings and bell ringings mingled with that wonderful Gallic cry *Attention! Attention* which is applicable to all emergencies from that of a child about to spill the milk to the Eiffel Tower about to fall. The little vessel backed water

furiously, came about at an angle like a contestant for the
America's Cup, and chugged up alongside again. Lines were
thrown across and everybody yelled at the top of their
lungs. Emily's French then was Bryn Mawr entrance re-
quirement, and she didn't understand what was being said
exactly, but she swears that a few seconds later someone
on our lower deck leaned perilously out across the inter-
vening space and solemnly handed something to a pompous
little French immigration official. Then everybody laughed
and one or two screamed *Merci infiniment!* and the tender
pulled away and steamed jauntily for shore. The object
of the commotion was a bottle of ink which the immigration official had had the unbelievable carelessness to leave
behind. He'd got it back now and everybody was happy.
Emily put her head down on the rail and cried again because the French were turning out just as she thought they
would.

She returned to our cabin and she says that Lord, I did
look awful! My face was swollen into the shape of the
harvest moon. It was the color of Chinese lacquer and it
glistened. Those spots were gathering but as yet hadn't
burgeoned, which was one reason I felt so wretchedly.
Emily told me to keep on holding them back, paralyzing
me with the threat that if I didn't the quarantine ward in
Hamburg was yearning for me. I lay there in misery trying
to control my rash and going over in my throbbing brain
what I could summon up of German declensions. I tried to
tell her where my things were but talking was too difficult
and I went off into momentary spells of feverish oblivion.
Through it all I was dimly aware of a little boy who kept
sticking his head in at our door and saying:

"Would you care to see the boots, Madam?"

"Boots?" Emily would answer, "No."

In a few minutes he'd be back again with the same question to which Emily would snap back the same re-- sponse, each time growing more irritated. The prospect of getting me off the ship had put her nerves on edge and at his fifth or sixth appearance she lost her temper.

"*No,*" she roared at the hapless child, "I don't want to see any boots! I don't ride and I don't fish and what I'd want boots for I can't imagine. And whatever shoe company has brought on board a collection has chosen a very peculiar time for it if you ask me."

I then realized what it was all about and sick as I was laughed till I cried.

"He's the 'Boots,' you zany!" I managed to say. "He's polished our shoes every day and the poor little devil wants a tip."

Emily said "Oh" somewhat crossly and gave it to him.

My one compensation in being ill was that Emily would have to shoulder the trying responsibility of tipping. I have never mastered the knowledge of the proper scale of tipping on a liner and I resent the whole idea. English stewards and stewardesses have a way of looking like earls and duchesses incognito and the thought of giving them a tip, call it a "gratuity" even, embarrasses me to such a point, I usually slip whatever I'm giving into a sealed envelope, hand it to them as if it were a valentine and run. If they are not the earl and duchess type, they're that mercurial variety who are all smiles when you get on board and sour-pusses when you land. Whatever you give them they won't like. If it's too little they look as if you'd robbed their child's bank and if it's too much they regard you with contempt, and if it's the proper amount they look dissatisfied on principle.

Luckily ours were the less aristocratic species of employee. The stewardess, a large motherly soul, helped dress me and the steward said to leave everything to him. We didn't know what that meant exactly but it sounded reassuring. One thing we were leaving him, at any rate, was a generous quantity of measle germs.

Joe Aub had left us at Cherbourg. Paul White and Emily, the only ones who knew my guilty secret, had to fix me up so I could pass the health inspector. From the sight of me this looked to be a task equivalent to fixing up a Rogers Group to pass for a Michelangelo. It was even doubtful if I'd get by with my passport picture. I struggled into my clothes, and with what negligible strength I had, tried camouflaging my face with slathers of foundation cream and half the contents of a box of face powder. The effect was that of someone who had been ducking for apples in a paper-hanger's bucket. This thick coating worked for a time but then the intense heat of my face baked it into a sort of dry *papier-maché* which, if I moved any facial muscle, cracked and revealed glimpses of that gleaming flesh. My parched lips I made up with one of those orange lipsticks which is supposed to change color once it's applied. It did, all right. Only instead of a delicate shade of coral, the medicine I'd been taking or something turned it into a lurid violet. With some curious notion that it would distract from the rest of my visage, I painted my mouth to look twice its normal size (and it's no sweetheart rosebud to begin with). Emily asked me gently if I wasn't being a bit spectacular and I said not at all, it was merely a case of understanding the art of the theatre, and that silenced her. The hat I selected to wear was a bright red number with a cock feather that swung down rakishly under my chin. I used to think it made me look rather like Irene Bordoni. But I didn't look like Irene Bordoni then. Fortunately for the dignity of the human race, I didn't look like anything that had ever before existed. If during the crossing, Emily and I, owing to our failure to whip up any feminine attachements, had earned the reputation of being scarlet women, I was certainly fixed up fine for the part. Emily and Paul, with saint-like tolerance, refrained from comment, nor did they say anything when I topped off my startling appearance with a flowing white veil which, I pointed out, would make me less conspicuous. I guess I'd gotten a little delirious by then.

We were nearing Southampton and a second wireless arrived from Mother and Father saying they'd be at the dock and couldn't wait to see us. Catching a glimpse of myself in the mirror, I wondered how they'd feel about waiting after they did.

Emily and Paul managed somehow or other to get me upstairs and into line for health inspection. They stood me between them so that in case I collapsed they'd be there to break my fall. I flashed a ghastly smile like a ballet-dancer's at the inspector, who merely shuddered and passed me as rapidly as possible. The passport gent never even looked up. The only persons who paid any attention to me were the other passengers who stared in bewilderment at the white veil and that art of the theatre make-up which gleamed through it. The ship by now was coming up to the dock and in half an hour we'd be ashore. I was propped against some cushions in a very dark corner of a deserted card room and told not to move, which, in view of the fact I scarcely could, seemed a superfluous admonition. For what seemed to me hours I sat there swathed in my white veil and utter wretchedness. Nobody came near me except a little girl who all at once skipped into the room, spied me and came to a dead stop. For some uneasy seconds she stood before me gazing with wonder. Then in an awed

whisper she said, "Do you tell fortunes?" and without waiting for an answer turned tail and ran.

Emily had gone out on deck to locate my parents. She didn't have much trouble. They were easily distinguishable, the darlings, there in the thick of the crowd staring up at the ship,—Father as if he'd been interrupted in the midst of reading and only half of him had come, and Mother like an excited little bird looking for us all over the vessel. She kept waving furiously at passengers who bore not the remotest resemblance to us, immigrants in the steerage, cooks in the galley, officers on the deck and she even blew a kiss or two at a lifeboat. Eventually she located Emily and pointed her out to Father, who had seen her for some time and had been waving intermittently in a vague but happy manner. Mother, cupping her mouth and standing on tiptoe as if that would make her voice carry higher, called out:

"Darling! Darling!" Then she added, "We've a surprise for you girls!"

"We've got a surprise for you too," Emily shouted back, and Mother again nodded with the tolerant smile one bestows on a child who comes up with a present of a mud pie. Then she and Father in unison sang out, "Where's Cornelia?"

This was the question Emily had been dreading, and having no answer for it she merely smiled and waved and pretended she hadn't heard. They halloed the question again and again but her only response was to wave and smile inanely. My parents gradually became aware that all was not as it should be. They recalled the experience of receiving that cryptic mid-ocean message saying that everything was all right and it had turned out to be a minor shipwreck. After the third demand, and Emily's third evasion, Father felt such nonsense had gone far enough and in a tone that made even the men on the bridge turn around, bellowed "WHERE IS CORNELIA???"

"Oh," Emily called back as lightly as she could and still be heard, "she's inside. She's got a little cold."

Mother turned pale and clutched Father's arm. "It's her appendix, Otis! I always knew her appendix would catch up with her!"

Father said nonsense, he didn't think it was my appendix at all but from his expression it was obvious he thought it might be anything from laryngitis to leprosy.

The gangplank was lowered, and down it Emily rocketed like a ball in a bowling alley, rushed straight up to Mother and Father, embraced them and said in the tense sotto-voce of a conspirator, "Don't say a word to anybody. Don't even whisper it because if it becomes known we are lost. But Cornelia has measles."

Whereat Father, in that voice which for fifty years thrilled the topmost occupant of the highest seat in the gallery, whooped "MEASLES!!!" and would have whooped it again only Mother, who had sized up the situation, deftly and discreetly put a hand with a handkerchief in it over his mouth.

"Where is she, Emily?" she asked quietly.

Emily told them they had me cooling in a dark corner, and that the doctor was with me. Telling Father to follow, Mother started up the gangplank. An officer told her she wasn't allowed on board and some able-bodied seamen held out restraining arms. What happened to them was what happened to anyone on whom Mother shed her charm. She just smiled at them, and in her beautiful voice murmured a lot of charming jargon that made no sense whatsoever . . . about her child and a friend . . . at Bryn Mawr together . . . just outside Philadelphia . . . they had lived there too but not recently . . . and they were all going in a motor somewhere, but that was a surprise for the dear children . . . so brave, too, although she hadn't approved of their being alone in the first place . . . but of course Miss Mary was a tower of strength. And somehow she got up the gangplank and onto the boat. People just gave way, a trifle dazed.

She was pretty dazed herself when she saw me and so I guess was Father for I still have a distinct picture of him staring at me with the same expression with which, as Macbeth, he must have stared at Banquo's ghost. Then, I remember, he collapsed onto a silly gilt chair and laughed till the tears ran down his cheeks. This hurt my feelings acutely and Mother was indignant with him and couldn't understand his callous glee. But he kept saying, "It's the make-up, Maud!" and he'd go off again into a fresh paroxysm. Perhaps it was just as well that he did, for Mother at sight of me had taken me in her arms and put my fantastic head on her soft little bosom, and in that gentle and familiar sanctuary I forgot about being Irene Bordoni or Theda Bara and would doubtless have sobbed my heart out if Father's wild hilarity hadn't cramped the style of my self-pity.

They led me onto the deck, where in the harsh light of day I looked a good deal worse. Bits of that facial calcimine had flaked off revealing the fact that those long-awaited spots were coming out. But somehow the four of them got me off the ship and onto the dock. Even on terra firma we weren't out of danger of discovery. I might still be nabbed and sent to an isolation ward of sorts. The plan was to go to the leading hostelry of Southampton acting as if nothing were amiss. Father and Emily would do the registering while Mother and Paul would follow with me, whisking me as swiftly as possible through the lobby and up to a quiet room without letting on to the innocent innkeeper and his guileless employees the horrid fact that they were harboring a not-so-distant relative of Typhoid Mary.

I put on really quite a commendable act; laughed and chatted giddily, passed the customs in a dazed but grand manner, and sprang with a spurt of super-human activity into a touring car the family had waiting there for us all. This was the surprise Mother had in store for us. She and Father had struck a bargain with the driver of an open Daimler, and in it we were to journey to London in leisurely fashion, stopping off at places of interest on the way. Heigh-ho! It was a pretty notion! We now journeyed from the dock to the hotel.

The hotel was one of those British terminal ones, part caravansary, part ticket office, right on the tracks, the sort that gives the impression of having engines running in and out of the potted palms. In the lobby I kept up my act of laughter and carefree abandon. We were allotted rooms, although the clerk gaped at me in my white veil and formidable complexion. But I carried it off, and didn't let down until I reached the room. There, once they got me in bed, I went completely and noisily delirious. And my but that was fun! With the porter and the chambermaid coming in and God knows who else, and me sitting up in bed with the art of the theatre sagging on my face but still lurid. My four attendants would close in around me as if I were giving them football signals, screening me as best they could, then trying to hold me down as soon as the coast was clear. At last the outsiders departed and with them the threat of being found out. I felt like a French aristocrat who had escaped the talons of the revolution, although the only one I remotely resembled was the Scarlet Pimpernell. I sank back on a burning pillow, and for the next few days I was awfully, awfully sick.

CHAPTER 5

PAUL WHITE stayed on in Southampton for a few days. When I think not only of his generosity in sacrificing so much of his holiday time, but of his saving me from that fate worse than death, the German quarantine camp, I am his for life at any time if he ever wants me (Dr. White of Boston please note). He made certain my rash had come forth as it should and that despite the risk involved in landing with a temperature of 102° I was not going to have pneumonia. Then he went on his way while the rest of us stayed on in that terminal hotel for ten mortal days and nights. Those ten days passed by only because days eventually do. The wearisome passage of time meant less to me than to the others. I just lay in an aching doze scarcely aware of what was going on around me. As a matter of fact, what was going on around me was no great shakes, for Emily, at any rate. Mother at least was kept busy nursing me and Father didn't especially mind this enforced halt in their travel itinerary as it gave him a chance to work on the script of next season's play. But poor Emily! Her introduction to Europe, that Europe over which she had cried with such tender appreciation, was anything but colorful. She had pictured her first night on English soil taking place in some quiet wayside inn, peaceful, quaint and of course thatched, where in a Jacobean bed in a dear little chintz-trimmed room she would drift off to sleep lulled by the tinkle of sheep-bells and the scent of hedgerows. Instead she found herself in a room which was in some way suspended out over the railroad tracks. What held it up was a mystery, unless possibly it rested on the bridge of a signal tower. Trains passed to and fro directly under the floor. She could open her window and get a bird's-eye view of a locomotive, to say nothing of some deep drafts of Welsh coal smoke. Engines puffed and shunted beneath her bed all night long, and when from sheer exhaustion she'd be dropping off to sleep, her ears and nerves would be suddenly shattered by the hysterical screech of a British whistle, which sounds like the whoop of an elderly spinster who has suddenly been pinched. If her nights were wakeful, her days were dreary dull. She'd wander down to the docks and gaze at the ocean liners, but even Cunarders can pall in interest after a while. Then she'd amble dolefully back to the terminal hotel for one of those meals which is to be had, thank God, only in terminal hotels. Too much has already been said and written by sassy Americans on the subject of the English commercial cuisine. Suffice it to say that Emily didn't like it either.

After a day or so, when he saw that his child in all probability wasn't going to die, Father eased the tedium of things for Emily by taking her on a few day trips, the New Forest, Winchester and such, which was a good thing from all points of view. Heretofore Emily had been pretty much awed and even a little terrified of Father. He in turn had regarded her as he regarded all my playmates, as creatures to be at once treated politely, and avoided as much as possible. Now, however, they became close and giddy buddies, a fact which filled me with that special and fatuous sort of pride you feel when your favorite people hit it off well, as if you'd done it all yourself. Emily's awe of

Father vanished into thin air, and when she was with him she relaxed her efforts at being sophisticated, and became less a *femme fatale* than a giggling school girl. And Father found Emily slightly mad, constantly amusing, and like no one he'd ever met before. They'd return from an outing in a state of hilarity. One could hear them coming from way down the length of the corridor. Father on entering my room would call out in clarion tones, "Where's my measly child?" or "How's the Spotted Peril?" and have to be frantically shushed by Mother.

The *Empress* stayed in port three days before going on to Hamburg. We had one *mauvais quart d'heure* when the ship's doctor, who possibly had had his suspicions all along, took it upon himself to send up his card saying he'd heard I'd been suffering from a slight cold and could he see me. I remembered the doctor as being aloof and impassive, like a forbidding version of C. Aubrey Smith. The prospect of undergoing his penetrating stare shot my temperature up. It was certain they'd found out about me. I recalled the rigid British quarantine laws regarding dogs, and began to think that maybe they applied to infected human beings as well, in which event I'd be held for six months in some place like Spratt's kennels, where my loved ones could visit me only on Sundays. But I was reckoning without Mother and her gentle wiles. She put on her prettiest hat, and with a radiant smile tripped down to greet the doctor and tell him all about her daughter . . . well, perhaps not quite all. A half hour later Emily and Father came upon them having tea amid the potted palms and engines. The Doctor was asking if he might show her about Southampton, that is, if her husband would trust her to an old dog like him—ha-ha!—an old sea-dog—ha-ha-ha!

In time my temperature subsided to normal, my rash faded away and none of those adult complications of a pulmonary or mastoid nature developed. In a week I was on my feet again, not that my feet were particularly good, and heaven knows my knees weren't any. But I flopped about, gradually gaining strength, and after three days of sunshine and Bovril, was sufficiently recovered for us all to depart for London in that open Daimler. Mother bundled me up so I could hardly breathe, and I don't remember being able to see at all. I was swaddled in mufflers and sweaters, and I had the further discomfort of being forced to wear Emily's appalling Canadian great-coat. I still felt awful and I think I must have looked awful too. But I struck a disgustingly gallant attitude, rather fancying myself an Elizabeth Barrett who was not long for this world. We stopped off at a number of points of interest and culture, most of which made little or no impression on me. I'm the uncivilized type who doesn't take in things unless I'm healthy. I do remember remaining overnight in Salisbury. Emily and my parents wandered diligently about the cathedral while I slumped on a seat in a posture of meditation trying to think about Gothic architecture but in reality brooding about whether it would be consumption or melancholia that would carry me off.

I felt better next morning. It was market day and the sight of those rosy-cheeked, smocked farmers who might have stepped out of a bright Moreland print, the thick fat sheep and the glorious thundering Clydesdales, their hooves heavy with umbrellas of hair, manes gay with straw and ribbon plaitings, and the biggest, roundest, most beautiful rumps in the entire animal kingdom, exuded an aura of health, and I found myself perking up and deciding I might, after all, last out the summer.

We visited the cemetery at Stoke Poges and took snap-shots of each other sitting with gingerly reverence on the tombstone of Thomas Gray. And we stopped off to see Stonehenge, and to have a picnic lunch amid those great inexplicable slabs which Emily kept calling "troglodytes," a name which strikes me as being as fitting for them as any other. The weather had been that average English June weather, which for the most part is terrible. It rained a lot, and the inns at which we stayed were dank and wintry and guiltless of any heat because people went on the theory that after all it was June and one didn't have heating in June, and if the weather chose to be beastly the only thing to do was pay no attention to it. I shook with constant chills, and Emily said she knew she was coming down with ague; she wasn't certain just what ague was but it sounded like something that would be a logical result of British weather. However, there were times when our discomfort would vanish like a bad dream; those were the times when the sun came out the way it does only in England. When one has reached the conclusion that it's the most wretched country on the globe the sun comes out just long enough to prove that it's the most beautiful. The car sped along in that giddy left-hand manner which makes you feel you must tap the chauffeur on the shoulder and say, "Over to the right, my good man," past hedgerows shining with re-cent rain and maytrees festive with bloom. One could hear the sweet, shrill music of larks, and we tried quoting "Hail to thee, blithe spirit," but couldn't get beyond "and soaring ever singest." Still we felt we were pretty intellectual and so did Mother; that is, she thought it was a step in the right direction. Houses became closer together, and the outline

of London hove into sight. Again we tried to quote something but I could only think of "Westminster Bridge"
and Emily kept muttering, "Childe Harold to the dark
tower came," to which Father rudely appended, "His co-
horts were gleaming with purple and gold." After which,
Mother said she thought we'd better stop trying.

Once arrived in London, we parted company with
Mother and Father. They had served their purposes during
my illness. Now I was recovered and "raring" to be independent again. They went their way (I daresay somewhat
secretly relieved, if truth were told) to their habitual caravansary, the hotel Victoria in Northumberland Avenue,
while Emily and I set forth for the more bohemian atmosphere of "lodgings." Through some colorful flight of fancy
we had made arrangements to take over the rooms of a
former Bryn Mawr student who had spent the previous
winter working for a Ph.D. at the University of London.
She was one of those brilliant scholars far too intellectual
to be concerned with creature comforts, and after we saw
the way she lived we came to the conclusion that we
weren't intellectual types after all. She had written us that
she was leaving for a "hiking" trip (that fine outdoor term
implicit of any number of splendid things in the way of
blisters, fish and chips and a brave avoidance of baths).
However, she assured us that the landlady was fully cogni-
zant of our arrival, and would be waiting for us with welcome at I forget what number Tavistock Square. As a
cheery afterthought she added she hoped we'd be happy in
her "digs," a word which slightly startled us and made us
wonder if we were to lodge in some sort of cellar.

The "digs," however, proved to be on the topmost floor
of an ancient manse which had been converted into a room-

ing house along about the beginning of the reign of Edward ,VII. It was situated in a part of London neither chic nor quaint, an extremely commonplace district somewhere back of the British Museum, and from the glimpses we caught of the other lodgers, it looked as if they'd come straight out of some of the cases. One toiled up four flights of extremely audible stairs and collapsed into our quarters consisting of two dreary, barren rooms which, when the residence had known better days, must have housed the tweenie and the second footman. One contained a bed, a studio couch and a washstand with an assortment of bowls, pitchers and soap dishes which didn't match, being for the most part souvenirs from Brighton and the Exhibition of 1854. We gathered this must be the bedroom and through the process of elimination came to the ingenious conclusion that the other was a sitting room, although it looked more like a semi-denuded storeroom. It contained a desk which had been made out of a grand piano, a couple of Morris chairs fancied up with anti-macassars, a small fireplace with a coal grate and a framed picture of Watts' "Hope," that dejected symbol of anything but. There was also a bookcase containing on the top shelf the Bryn Mawr scholar's text books, which were so erudite we couldn't understand even their titles, and on the lower shelf a brass alcohol lamp and a teapot shaped like a duck or some such whimsey. The landlady had gone off for a holiday up the Thames and we were left to the tender mercies of a cockney slavey. She'd clatter in at seven A.M. to fix the one fire we had all day, then at seven-thirty she'd charge back with a pitcher of hot water, which in London June weather didn't stay hot very long. At eight she'd bring us a tasty breakfast, half an orange for each, fried eggs and leathery bacon, a pot of that witch's brew they call coffee, and some slabs of toast arranged in an open-air rack to insure their being nice and cold. When we petitioned ever so meekly permission to receive these blessings a trifle later in the day, she said, "Carn't, Miss. Mrs. 'Iggins's horders." Some mornings we'd say to hell with Mrs. Higgins and breakfast, and turn over for a couple of hours more sleep; but during such periods of oblivion the water would have become the glacial temperature of the room, and the fire would have gone out. Starting the fire required a knack known only to the slavey, who miraculously got those bits of damp kindling and chunks of igneous rock ignited by spreading out a newspaper across the fireplace and blowing vociferously. We'd try that, too, but the only thing to ignite would be the newspaper and one of us would have to come running with a water pitcher to put out the conflagration, not that a conflagration could have made much headway in that room. This commotion would rouse the slavey, who would poke her face in the doorway and say severely that Mrs. 'Iggins wouldn't 'arf be put out, which was her simple homespun way of implying that if we persisted in such tricks we'd be the ones who'd be put out.

The bathroom was down two flights of stairs, and that involved some interesting encounters with the other tenants, all of whom seemed to be elderly gentlemen in conservative bathrobes, carrying towels, shaving mugs and copies of the *Daily Mail*. Emily nearly knocked one down the stairs one morning, and to hide her confusion spoke to him in her most friendly Indiana way. But he gave her the disdainful look he must in his younger days have cast at a Piccadilly *fille de joie* and shot for sanctuary through the nearest door.

The first morning in this giddy establishment Emily, who

had been holding converse with the slavey, said to me, "There's some queer sort of character who lives in this house."

"Queer?"

"Yes," she said, "that girl just told me. He's apparently some sort of old eccentric, and when you see him you have to tip him."

"Just what did the girl say?" I asked.

"She said, 'You'll have to look out for the geezer, Miss. It's always best to have tuppence handy for the geezer.'"

I felt this to be another of Emily's original flights of fancy, but what it meant didn't dawn on me until I went down for my bath. The water for the tub was heated by one of those little gas-jet arrangements which flicker beneath a small copper boiler. After a time, if you're lucky, a forlorn trickle of hot water dribbles forth, cooling off considerably before it hits the tin tub below. I remembered this was called a *geyser* and went back upstairs to tell Emily so. She became indignant as she always does when she's misunderstood a thing.

"Then why don't they call it a geyser?" she snapped.

"They do. Only they pronounce it geezer."

"I suppose they call Old Faithful a water-pistol!"

The geezer was a mercenary contraption. There was a slot into which one dropped two coppers to pay for the gas. When twopence worth was consumed the gas went out. We were informed that if this occurred when we were still running the water, we must immediately insert two more coins in the slot. If we didn't, the slavey prophesied, "everythink might blow hup." I well remember one morning when, as I was disporting myself like a dolphin in a couple of inches of tepid water, the gas gave a blue spurt, and with a little dying hiccough went out completely. The room was of that bracing June chill and I hadn't even started soaping myself. I yelled to Emily to bring me some more coins. She didn't have any coppers in her purse, but she came down the stairs two at a time with a sixpence. All this accomplished was merely to drop down the slot and onto the floor without in any way rousing the gas. I recalled the slavey's warning about the thing blowing up unless, like Mammon, you kept it stoked with coins. Odd rumblings were issuing from the little copper boiler. Emily, always active if not always logical in an emergency, cried, "Don't move, darling!" and pushed me back into the chilly water. She dashed downstairs, but couldn't find a living soul. The slavey had vanished, and those elderly gentlemen,

the other lodgers, had either gone to business or were hiding behind locked doors. She stepped out onto the street in search of a shop or even a flower vendor who might make change. But Tavistock Square is guiltless of any shops. They haven't a newsstand. Then a bus pulled up beside her, and that seemed to solve the problem. Hatless and coatless, she jumped on the back platform, got change for two and

six, rode one block and jumped off murmuring to the bewildered conductor, "You see, my friend is up there stark
naked with the geezer and I have to hurry back to her,"
which straightened everything out nicely. By the time she
returned I had turned quite blue with cold, but Old Faithful had not yet erupted.

For all that little financial lesson in the Montreal hotel,
Emily was still confused by British currency. She'd grown
highly incensed not only with it but with me because she
couldn't understand it. (It was the only thing I ever heard
her admit to not understanding.) It was in vain that I tried
to show her the difference between a half-crown and a two
shilling piece. She refused to admit they were anything but
two versions of fifty cents and persisted in being so stub-
bornly obtuse about it I finally told her if she'd just bring
herself to read what was written on them she'd know.
This didn't work out so well either, because she'd keep
taxi drivers waiting interminably while she'd scan the reading matter of each and every coin, turning it round and
round, sometimes breathing on it and rubbing it clear.
When I suggested that people might think her awfully
queer she said not at all, they'd merely mistake her for a
coin collector. I tried explaining to her that "one florin"
meant two shillings but that only made her madder. The
day we received a bill made out in guineas, and I told her
that there was no such thing as a guinea, it was a pound
and one shilling, only the swanker shops charged you in
guineas, and you paid in pounds and shillings, but you
called it guineas although, as I had said, there really was no
such thing, she slapped me.

That was the summer when white fur evening wraps
were the rage. One saw them everywhere. They ranged

from chic models of dazzling ermine to cheap copies in rabbit. Some of the cheaper ones weren't too bad, or maybe
they were bad, all right, but a few smart women wore
them, and to us they spelled enchantment. The only fur
coat I'd ever had was made of what the salesgirl had vowed
was "mountain lion" but what wore into a substance more
like circus lion and a retired one at that, while Emily's
was a cutdown squirrel of her mother's. As for evening
wraps, the best I could boast was a tasty mandarin jacket,
while Emily still clung to the green velvet cloak Grand-
mother Kimbrough had brought her from the San Fran-
cisco Exposition. We felt that if ever the day arrived when
we could afford white fur evening wraps we'd believe in
fairy godmothers. Then suddenly the day arrived when we
found we could. Emily out for a solitary stroll one morning had spied a shop whose window displayed a vision of
rabbit splendor marked £6–10s–6d. She had a feeling this
was within our humble means, but not being quite certain,
she rushed back to our dovecote to ask me what "El six,
ten esses and six dees" meant. With the then rate of exchange it was about the equivalent of $30. We lost no
time, rushed to the shop and without a moment's hesita-
tion bought a couple, one each, and exactly alike. That was
the incredible era of shapeless dresses and shapeless wrap-
around coats with voluminous sleeves and rolled collars.
Our models were capes, and as I recall them now they must
have been daisy-bells. Made of snowy rabbit (we were later
to discover it was not only white but flying) they were
fashioned along the lines of a tent, adorned with a deep
yoke and an even deeper object known as a "cape collar."
They were perfectly enormous and we could wrap them
about us twice with a d'Artagnan flourish which we

thought was chic and gave us a worldly air. Not daring to entrust these treasures to a delivery boy, we ourselves

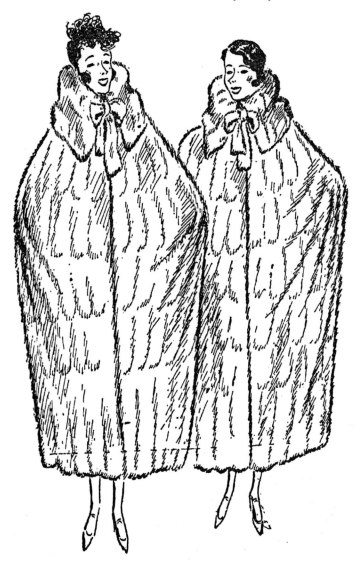

lugged them in huge boxes back to our lodgings where we spent a lot of time parading in them before a large and pallid mirror hanging above the washstand.

expensive we hadn't been able to buy any others since. Then, wrapping the great bell-shaped cloaks about us, we set forth from the lodging-house feeling like personifications of Queen Marie of Roumania and Peggy Hopkins Joyce. We had to walk a block or two before we found a taxi. It was one of those evenings characteristic of the London season, when one goes out to dinner in broad daylight. People stared at us somewhat but we didn't mind. We thought it was because we looked so dazzling. We may have looked dazzling, but we also looked like a pair of igloos out for a stroll. We spied a taxi, hailed it and gave with a good deal of grandeur the address of the Trocadero. As we clambered in I rather received the impression that the driver said, "Right you are, Snowball," but decided I must be mistaken. Fearful of harming our new and spotless purchases by sitting on them, we pulled them out from under us, and held them up gingerly about our midriffs and shoulders. The things rose in the breeze and billowed out, filling all available space. We were pretty well snowed under. The taxi came to a stop before the Trocadero, and laboriously we began working our way out of the fur clouds. Getting out of a taxi is not one of life's nimbler activities under the easiest of conditions, but to get out when weighted down by a white fur pup-tent was a feat indeed. We emerged in jack-knife posture, managed to make the pavement on our feet and not our foreheads, shook ourselves out and paid the cabman, who was grinning broadly in what we never doubted was admiration. Then I caught sight of Father. He was waiting for us outside the restaurant. But for some curious reason he was leaning against the wall, and for an even more curious reason tears were running down his face. He looked to be hysterical. I couldn't imagine what was the matter. Emily, who didn't know him so well, thought that he must be in the throes of some unfathomable mood inherent in a great actor, and that whatever might be causing it, the radiant vision of the two of us would bring him out of it pretty quick. We smiled at him and waved graciously the way we thought Mary Garden might. At this he covered his face with a handkerchief and shook as if he were in the throes of some sort of malarial chill. We looked at one another with blank amazement and Emily hissed, "What's making him take on so?" It never remotely entered our vaguest suspicions that we might have something to do with it. We approached him shyly and were about to inquire softly if there were anything we might do, when he looked out from behind the handkerchief and we realized his tears were due to wild, uncontrollable laughter.

"Oh, my God!" he managed to choke forth. "How could you get so *many* rabbits!" We couldn't believe our ears. "And what," he went on, "in the name of dear, sweet, gentle heaven was that *can-can mouvement* you were doing in the taxi with your skirts up over your heads?"

I was deeply offended and said *"Father!"* in a crushing tone, but he continued being anything but crushed. He led the way into the restaurant and we followed, still trying to look like Mary Garden, but with an uncomfortable hunch that maybe what we most closely resembled were *Flopsey* and *Mopsey* in *Peter Rabbit*. Mother had seen our entrance and by the time we reached the table she was in a condition of hysteria similar to Father's. We were hurt and quite bewildered. The only consoling thing was the fact that Mother was too weak to become cross over my extravagance, and she did agree that it was a *great deal* of fur for $30.00.

They treated us to champagne that evening, which did a lot to soothe our wounded pride. And as a further aid to reëstablishing our self-confidence, Father ordered some especially old Courvoisier. Emily at the sight of the large brandy glass said, "Mercy! I won't be able to drink that big a glassful!" She could never forget her great-grandmother Curry, who shortly after the Civil War had pulled off a spectacular buggy-ride in record time to open the first prohibition campaign in Ohio. She was relieved but also somewhat disappointed when the wine captain poured out a dab which barely covered the bottom. That dab had its effect, however, for after sipping and sniffing it for a time she said she guessed she'd had enough because the room was starting to go round. Father said that was all right, when it came time for us to go home all she'd have to do would be to go across to Trafalgar Square, sit on one of the lions and wait till Tavistock Square came round.

We spent our time sight-seeing, buying dozens of postcards we never sent and sponging off the family as many free meals as possible. Life was pleasant and would have been perfect had we not been obliged to start and end up each day in that doleful lodging house. To be sure, we were being independent, but we began to think that as far as creature comforts were concerned, independence wasn't so hot (and when I remember the temperature of those rooms the word is apt.) The family suggested ever so delicately that we might like to change to their hotel and we leapt at the chance like hungry trout to a succulent fly. We moved into a small but comfortable room near them and once securely no longer on our own, began again to feel mondaine. We dressed for dinner every night, which set us up all right. Occasionally Mother and Father blew us to the theatre. We'd wear our white fur coats, the shock of which had worn off by now, and try to appear blasé and if ever we encountered people we knew, which was likely, as half of America was over there that summer, we'd come out with offensive remarks to the effect that there was nothing like London during the Season, was there? Father took us on a few tours about town, showing us places he'd known and loved when he'd played there thirty years before with the Daly Company. He was especially fond of an old cemetery for actors. It was in a shoddy out-of-the-way district and the ground was unhallowed. Even in death, members of the profession were ostracized, because until well after the Restoration they were legally considered "Rogues and Vagabonds," not fit to lie with gentle folk. That pleased him highly. It was evident he felt it a sorry day when players turned respectable. One day Mother, who had read in the *Times* that the Royal Family was to leave for the country at eleven, scuttled us off to Buckingham Palace to watch the departure. We stood along with a handful of governesses and casual passers-by—nobody else seemed to have made an occasion of it—when the gates opened and the Family appeared, rather crowded into one car like any other family starting for the station. The few men around us took off their hats, the nannies pointed out the car to their children, and Emily and I just looked. But not Mother. Not for nothing had she assisted on the stage the entrance of Kings and Queens. She fluttered to the ground in a deep, 18th Century curtsey, spreading as wide as possible the

skirt of her tailored suit. We looked down at her in amazement. We weren't the only ones amazed—Queen Mary
nearly fell out of the car.

The family received a constant stream of callers and
whenever we thought them sufficiently well-known we'd
horn in if possible. One afternoon Sybil Thorndike was
to come to tea, also Gilbert Miller. The prospect of meeting Gilbert Miller made me rather twittery. I was about
to launch forth upon the stage and, who knew, Mr. Miller
might offer me a job if I made an impression on him. It
seemed a golden opportunity. They arrived and their visit
passed pleasantly. Also a decided impression was made on
Mr. Miller, but not by me. My thunder was stolen by
Emily, who in her excitement over this distinguished occasion ate the pink baby-ribbon which was tied around the
sandwiches. It was hard to chew and even harder to swal-
low because it got untied in transit and she had to gulp
it down like a stomach-pump. But to pull it out hand over
hand would have been even more spectacular, so she washed
it down with tea, hoping it wouldn't start tying itself in
bowknots around her appendix. Gilbert Miller never took
his eyes off her. He never even blinked. And as for topping
that impression, I hadn't a chance.

CHAPTER 6

MOTHER decided one day that it would be part of our cultural education to go Old English and take the coach trip to Hampton Court. She had looked it all up in Muirhead's Guide Book and it sounded to be a thrill at once picturesque and distinguished. One rode on the swaying top of a tally-ho behind four spanking greys, or maybe they were bays, while Lord Somebody drove. This opportunity for displaying four-in-hand skill was, we learned, a pastime of the peerage and a few horsey American millionaires who, in the interests of tradition, kept up the old mail-coach service between London and Hampton Court. Two or three times a week the members of this sporting hierarchy took turns driving the romantic vehicle just for the hell of it, and the bourgeoisie, consisting chiefly of American tourists, could purchase places on it and go along for the ride. It was well known in advance who would drive, and if you were the sort who went in for such simple pleasures as getting into close, if not speaking proximity to nobility, you could ascertain in advance that if you made the trip of a Tuesday Lord Diddle-de-boom would drive you, while if you went on Friday your safe-conduct would be in the competent hands of the Earl of Whatsis. The Americans, I believe, weren't scheduled; they just served as subs, paid for the privilege and scrambled in whenever some nobleman's gout canceled his appearance.

I've forgotten what peer it was who drove the day we

went. All I remember about him is that he looked like Rudyard Kipling. Mother, who along with Muirhead's guide had been perusing society pictures in the weekly

periodicals and tid-bits out of the Court Register, knew all about him. He was frightfully posh and although Mother's Jeffersonian simplicity never allowed her to admit it, she was always secretly deeply impressed by such deities. I think that on this occasion she rather fancied herself sitting in quiet dignity beside Lord Whoever-he-was or if not beside him, then not far away, and maybe before the drive was over we'd all be asked to tea at his ancestral hall or, who knew? to his country seat for the shooting. But it didn't work out quite that way. The only person who sat beside that notable was his groom or assistant pilot, or perhaps it was his whipper-in since his chief activity seemed to be to hold a whip and shoo us all into our seats and then give the signal or the halloo or whatever to his Lordship. Our seats were well in the back and the only time his Lordship looked in our direction at all was just before the start when he rose and slowly turned round in order to wrap himself in a driving-apron which his man helped wind about him, and if he saw us then he never let on.

Coaching is fun, I guess. At least we tried to act as if it were. We felt awfully high up and shockingly exposed on those lofty seats, and God knows there was plenty of atmosphere. It was rather terrifying because there was nothing to hold on to except a little armrest the size and shape of half a croquet wicket and it wasn't any too solid. Lord Whatsis drove the careening equipage at Pony Express speed, rounding corners at such an angle the only thing that kept us from flying off must have been some sort of centripetal force. We dashed headlong down London's busiest thoroughfares, Rudyard Kipling never changing expression at near collisions with taxis, motor lorries and on-coming busses. Every now and then a liveried servant who appeared to be suspended in mid-air behind us, although it turned out he was hanging on by means of a coping and a sort of subway strap, would let off a deafening blast on three yards of brass horn, warning traffic for the love of heaven to get out of the way, and by some miracle we got through without losing a wheel or running over any small children, which ever since I read "The Tale of Two Cities" I thought coaches always did.

Once we were clear of the city and traffic danger, the skies proceeded to oblige with one of those cloudbursts the British in their joking way call a sudden shower, and that was fun too. The morning had dawned with warm and brilliant sunshine, and being trusting souls, we had believed the papers, which said "Fair," and weren't dressed for rain. We huddled together like sheep in a blizzard, and the whipper-in, taking compassion on us, handed us some huge funereal umbrellas; but the wind nearly pulled them with us attached to the handles out into space. So we just sat there and tried to accept the rain like grateful flowers, and to ignore the fact that water was running down our necks and that the patterns of our summer prints were soaking off onto our skins like decalcomanias.

The sun came out when we reached Hampton Court and that made everything all right. We went about dutifully appreciating everything. In those days we worked hard and conscientiously at appreciation and kept it up pretty well unless we tried to over sight-see and came down with acute cases of "museum legs." But at Hampton Court we didn't have to work very hard. Appreciation fairly broke over us in unevoked waves at the sight of those showrooms that made one resolve to brush up on English history (not that the resolve is ever carried out), the forests of chimney-pots, the brick walls bordered with wet spicy box, and those breath-taking gardens, the sort that have helped make English poetry the glory that it is. And in amid the Tudor magnificence the touching little doorways with their polished brass plates . . . Lady So-and-So, the Hon. Mrs. Somebody Else. Apartments of "Grace and Favor" loaned by the King in his bounty to the needy aristocracy.

And then we came to the maze, or labyrinth. It was my idea to go into it. Emily was perfectly content to view its outer wall of centuries-old box, realize that it was a maze and let it go at that. But mine was the spirit of Raymond Whitcomb that day and I persuaded Emily to come along because, I said, we might be missing something. What we nearly missed was the train home. We went in, the green walls closed behind us and for a time we strolled along the paths still doing our appreciating and exchanging commendably cultural comments, speculating about the notable persons who had once trod the same ground, and wondering if Henry VIII had ever chased any of his wives around these tortuous lanes and if he'd ever gotten lost. There isn't much variety to a maze, just endless continuations of the same paths which twist about or end in cul-de-sacs. This being an ancient one, the hedge-walls were at least fifteen feet high, so while it's nice and instructive to learn that box can grow that high, there was a certain sameness to the passing scene. It wasn't long before we'd had enough and we started to go out. Then we realized that Henry VIII wasn't the only one who might have gotten lost. We were, as completely as if we'd been caught in Mammoth Cave with all the lights out. For half an hour we tramped about trying to find an exit, with as much success as squirrels in a cage. We were the only people in the place and we became rather uneasy. So did Mother and Father, who all the time were waiting on a bench outside. It seemed an interminably long time for us to have been gone, and they began to wonder if we'd met with some sort of disaster. Maybe there was a Minotaur at the center of this labyrinth too. Now and then they could catch the sound of our voices and Mother in an effort to be helpful would chirp from time to time, "Girls! Girls! Are you all right?" But as she was running around on the outside and calling from different vantage points, we couldn't tell from which direction her chirping was coming. We couldn't tell anything except that we were going round and round and rapidly getting nowhere. It wasn't possible to steer by the sun because that orb, as if to hide its embarrassment, had gone behind a cloud and we had the further diversion of being inundated by another of those sudden summer showers. We became extremely cross with each other. I snapped at Emily that as long as we were in there she might at least look about her and not keep her eyes glued angrily to the ground. She snapped back that there was nothing to see but box and she'd had enough of that to last her a lifetime; moreover, the reason she was watching the ground was in order to identify the puddles through which we were sloshing. It might be a means of finding our way out. I asked how, and she said that if we went through the same puddle twice it would at least prove something. I asked what it would prove, and after that we didn't talk. We must have tramped about that wretched boxwood jungle for forty-five minutes. We grew panic-stricken and felt like the Emperor Jones in the last act. We were pretty well exhausted, Emily even more so than I because she was wearing the Canadian tweed coat. There was no Paul White to hold it up for her by the back of the neck, and her knees were sagging. Just as we were beginning to wonder if they'd have to send bloodhounds out after us, a guard appeared on a look-out platform which towered above the hedge walls, and started to yell at us in a rather inhuman manner. He said we'd been in there way too long, which was hardly news to us; that the time allotted visitors was up and to please come out. We yelled back that if he could get us out we'd never take another minute of their precious time, not as long as we lived. Cupping his hands into a megaphone he called out directions to us, telling us to take this turn, then that, then go back, then forward—it was like pacing the combination of a safe—and finally we emerged, wet, irritable and dizzy.

Outside we found Mother and Father. They were wet and irritable too. They'd been sitting on that bench in the pouring rain all the time except when Mother had made her spasmodic little chirping trips. Somebody suggested tea and we all brightened at the thought, Mother in particular because she said we could eat a high tea and not bother about dinner. That was one of her favorite economies, proposed if seldom carried out, and she kept on proposing it despite the fact that Emily and I had never had a tea high enough to deter us from eating a roaring dinner just as soon as we could get at it. However, we always encouraged her in this little illusion because in the end it provided us with two large meals. The rain was coming down in torrents. Drenched and soaked, we scuttled across to a quaint-looking inn which hung precariously over the green bank of the Thames. The door was open but there wasn't a living soul inside. Tables were set, but there was nobody to wait on them. A fire was laid in a vast fireplace but it wasn't going. The only appreciable difference between the room and the weather outside was that the moisture wasn't being precipitated in rain water. Otherwise it was just as cold and damp. We divested ourselves of our outer and wetter garments but nobody came to hang them up for us. Drenched with rain and jibbering with cold, we longed desperately to start the fire but there were no matches and we hadn't brought any. Father had only his lighter which had never been known to light, but which he felt he ought to carry occasionally because Mother had given it to him. We cleared our throats, pulled bell-cords, banged doors, called "Waiter!" and even "Garçon!" but nothing happened. I started sneezing and Father did some impressive coughing, while Mother, not to be outdone, began making depressing little remarks about us all coming down with something. It was at that precise moment of despair that Emily emitted a cry of joy and announced that she and she alone could save the day for us. She had found in her purse a box of matches. We could start the fire, light cigarettes, get warm and dry and nobody need come down with anything. We were relieved and delighted, and Mother in her most lavish way said, "Now wouldn't Emily be the one to have just the right thing when we most needed it!" a remark I thought rather unnecessary of her. To find herself suddenly so essential was a novel experience for Emily. She beamed and muttered with fatuous modesty, "The only one to have any matches!" The fire was the most urgent business at hand, and like a Campfire Girl to the rescue, she knelt before it. She opened the box and striking a match with fine flourish held it out eagerly but not too effectively. Nothing happened. It was a burned match, it had been burned before she'd tried to light it. She struck another. That, too, was burned. She tried a third with similar lack of result. Then staring blankly, she opened out the box and dumped the contents on the hearth. Every match was a burned one. To this day she doesn't know what she was doing with a box of burned matches, where she had found it, or who had stoked the box. We put away our cigarettes and without further comment sat dankly about the dead fireplace until, after what seemed days, a waiter finally appeared bringing with him a box of matches that weren't burned. We had tea . . . high, followed a few hours later in London by dinner . . . large. Toward the finish of the latter, Father after gazing at Emily for some time said, "Emily, I've come to the conclusion that you lie awake at night and just think these things up." We laughed, but his words apparently worried her. As we went to bed she turned to me and said quite seriously, "I don't really think, you know."

_____

Father had met H. G. Wells in Switzerland a year or two before the war. Each had gone there for a walking trip, and after encountering one another at numerous inns and beside various glaciers, they eventually exchanged cards on the summit of an Alp, since which time they had kept up an intermittent exchange of letters. The "Outline of History" was a best seller that year and I thought it was awfully distinguished of Father to be on correspondence terms with its author. My pride in my parent increased considerably when the great man wrote inviting us all to spend Sunday at his country place. He lived down at Dunmow, or maybe it was *up* at Dunmow (with London, as in the case of Maine, I never remember whether one goes *up* or *down* to it). We could, he said, get there by train, although the motor trip of some twenty miles or so was very pretty. After a careful survey of the family finances we decided the occasion warranted hiring a car. Even Mother agreed. This, after all, was one of those extravagances which came under the heading of culture.

We all arrayed ourselves in our best. Emily and I had

notions that Sunday at an English country house called for
sport clothes. But the only ones we had were the baby blue
outfit of mine and Emily's Shakespearean tweed, and after
a visit to Fortnum and Mason we'd begun to have our
doubts about them. Accordingly, we fixed ourselves up in
our crêpe marocains. Emily's was dark blue and mine, I'm
afraid, was black. Emily's hat was a smart little milan straw
while mine, I'm further afraid, was that red Irene Bordoni
gem with the cock feather swooshing down across my chin.
We both wore high heels and I added the further exotic
touch of some earrings I had purchased in a Brompton
Road antique shop. They were dark tortoise-shell, carved
like Egyptian urns, and I thought them beautiful. I even
thought myself rather beautiful when I wore them, but I
wasn't. Thin and hollow-cheeked, my face, which was already too long, with these dangling appendages took on
the proportions of a primitive Greek horse.

It was a beautiful day and the drive through the smiling
countryside was heavenly. Our chauffeur, who was in-
clined to be loquacious, got so enthusiastic pointing out
passing sights of interest he missed a few important turn-
ings, and after a bit we found ourselves quite lost amid the
winding avenues of a vast estate. We drove past miles of
moor and woodland, through forests cleared of all under-
brush where giant trees that might have shaded the Plantag-
enets rose from a tidy green carpet of moss, fern and ancient lawn. Herds of fallow deer grazed in the open fields
or rested in the cool bracken, and just to make the setting
complete, some stately peacocks crossed our path. We
stopped a man on a bicycle who told us it was Lord Somebody's Park. Emily said it wasn't at all like McCullough
Park back in Muncie which in lieu of herds of deer boasted

one moth-eaten Rocky Mountain elk. It was all very lovely only, as Mother pointed out, it was already one o'clock, the hour we'd been asked for lunch, and we were still miles from Dunmow. When finally we turned in at Mr. Wells' gate it was almost two-thirty. We were all decidedly embarrassed, and Emily and I were not only embarrassed but suddenly horribly awed. Emily said it had just come over her all of a heap that she was about to meet Mr. H. G. Wells and she hadn't planned what she'd say to him.

"I can't meet Mr. Wells!" she cried. "Not till I've thought, anyway," and she slid down onto the floor of the car as it came to a stop and saying, "I'll just stay out of sight until I can collect myself," she went into a curious crouching position like a praying mantis. At that moment the door behind her was flung open and she bulged out rear first into Mr. Wells himself, so the formality of a conventional introduction was side-stepped. Mother tried to ease the situation with one of her charming streams of incoherencies to the effect that this was her daughter's friend Emily Kimbrough and she guessed she must be looking for something she'd dropped and the chauffeur had lost the way and we were so mortified to be so late.

She needn't have bothered, as Mr. Wells didn't appear to be in the least surprised. I guess he thought all Americans were crazy, anyway. He was shorter than I'd anticipated, but broad-shouldered and very stocky. The most surprising thing about him was his voice. From the looks of that burly neck one expected it to be a roar; instead, it came out in a sort of high-pitched tone which occasionally broke as if it were changing. He was cheery and full of welcome and the Lord knows replete with teeming vitality. One was instantly aware of it; not nervous restlessness, but bursting energy inadequately harnessed and rarin' to go.

He herded us into the house explaining that they'd finished lunch. Mother tried again to say that we'd gotten lost
but he wouldn't let her. Talking a steady stream, he bustled
us into the dining-room, set plates before us, went to the
sideboard to cut some beef, found it already cut, waved to
a young man who had drifted in, a gesture which seemed
to imply that he was to put the beef on our plates, pulled
out a chair beside Emily, hurtled himself into it and said:

"Now, young lady, tell me all about what you do. What
do you like? Do you read? What sort of things? Are you
educated? How old are you? What part of America do
you come from? Marvelous place, America. Ever been to
Hollywood? The coming intellectual and artistic center of
the world. Greatest commercial center now. Do you like
roast beef?"

He didn't give her time to answer all his questions but
she did manage to talk to him. She had had a job in a Buffalo book shop for a few months and that background gave
her the courage to discuss with him books, publishers and
authors. Mr. Wells talked with her as if she had been a
contemporary and she played up wonderfully well. She
knew all about the latest editions of the "Outline" and her
tactful references to that went far to make up for her awkward preliminary and somewhat backward encounter with
its distinguished author. The rest of us ate and listened
avidly. Occasionally he'd turn the mill-race of his conversation in our direction but it was aimed for the most part
at Emily. In his enthusiasm he'd lean so close to her face
she'd have to hold her fork with the roast beef on it well
off to one side until he'd made his point. I never heard more
brilliant summings up, opinions and epithets and we wish

we'd written it all down that night after we got back to London, because we've forgotten his exact words. What we do remember, apart from the tumbling exuberance of it, was his generosity toward other writers. He would quote with admiration a phrase from one author, an idea from another; he would speak almost with awe of the scope of this novelist, the sense of color of that one. He couldn't say enough, I remember, about James Harvey Robinson's "Mind in the Making."

From time to time he'd break off to ask if we were all getting enough to eat. During one of these intervals Mother cooed, "Your son makes a very good butler, Mr. Wells." The young man who had been waved toward the roast beef had in some way been identified as a son.

"Yes," said Mr. Wells. "He gets butler and butler every day," and he squealed happily over his wit. This made me feel better and Mother laughed tactfully, but Father, who was always embarrassed by puns unless they were of his own making, hastened to cover up such a lapse in a great man by enquiring:

"Are you a Cambridge man like your son?"

Mr. Wells screeched more happily than ever. "Lord, no, man! At his age I was a draper's assistant! But I'm going to send him to Hollywood. He'll make money there."

We got through lunch quickly. Emily had really outdone herself and although she had again proved her superiority to me, I was bursting with pride for her. It was obvious she was somewhat giddy about herself. Luncheon finished, she rose feeling, she later said, like the Comtesse de Noailles or some such glamorous intellectual. Mr. Wells pulled out her chair from which she turned with a willowy swoop and a brilliant smile for our host, intending to sweep on away from the table. There was a crash and a sort of whizzing sound, and instead of sweeping on away from the table she stood stock still, looking less like the Comtesse de Noailles than Lot's wife.

"Good God!" Mr. Wells said. "What have you done?" Emily said she didn't know but it felt as if she'd been caught in some sort of trap, at which Mr. Wells said, "Ah yes, the electric table-bell." It was the sort that is attached from the floor to the table-edge by a cord. In that willowy swoop of hers she had in some way hooked her toe in a loop and snapped the bell off its mooring with such violence the released wire had whipped itself in coils about her leg from ankle to knee, like an Elizabethan cross-garter, which, being still attached to the floor, held her immovable. Mr. Wells, equal to every occasion, was equal even to the sort Emily conjures up. For a moment he looked at her in astonishment, then pulled his glasses from his pocket and fitted them carefully on his nose. After which he got down on his hands and knees, lifted the tablecloth, crawled under and set to work unwinding. Mother stood by making little mooing noises of distress, Father looked on with amused compassion, while I smothered my face in a portière to keep Mr. Wells from hearing my maniacal yells of rapture.

He got her unwound, crawled out from under the table and straight over to Mother, rose and escorted her with dignity into the library, where Mrs. Wells, whom we then met for the first time, was entertaining the more punctual guests. We were more or less introduced to people. That is, Mr. Wells would lead us up to someone and without bothering about introducing anybody would start talking, or rather, continue talking. There was another American present, Mrs. Sanger, better known as Mrs. Birth Control

Sanger. Mr. Wells said she was crusading for a noble cause and Emily and I, who hadn't the remotest idea what Birth Control even meant, said, Yes, indeed, wasn't she? He then led us over to a very distinguished looking gentleman with a shock of white hair and said in his falsetto rush of words, "This is the greatest educationalist in all England. Do you know what an educationalist is?" And that was the nearest approach we got to an introduction to him. We never did learn his name, although we felt pretty sure it wasn't Bertrand Russell. There were also present two young men, obviously Cambridge buddies of Wells, Jr. (or do they call it Minor in England?). They were very pink cheeked and healthy and they answered to a couple of those appalling British nicknames like Bubble and Squeak. Only now that I remember, I believe people addressed them as Bungy and Poodles. They were later joined by a third young man whom Mr. Wells with happy laughter over his own humor called "Face." We wondered why. There was nothing out of the ordinary about that portion of the young man's anatomy, but Face he was called, and the other young men chortled heartily and said it was a jolly good name for him too.

We had no sooner got comfortably seated than one of those summer showers began its deluge outside. That was Mr. Wells' cue for jumping to his feet and announcing, "Now we'll all go out and play the Wells game!" Emily and I were sunk with horror. Was it for this we'd rigged ourselves up in our best city finery? Mrs. Wells, seeing our expressions and realizing that Americans are made of less waterproof stuff than Britons, tactfully suggested to her husband that it was raining, dear. To which he cheerfully replied that that being the case we could play on the indoor court. Our despair deepened. Emily remembered all too clearly her deck-tennis débâcle and as for me, the mere thought of any game more active than Twenty Questions made me sick at my stomach. Besides, how could we hope to move with any agility in those high heels and tight fitting crêpe dresses? We murmured that much as we were dying to play, we weren't dressed for it. But that didn't in the least deter Mr. Wells, who squealed happily that Mrs. Wells had an extensive collection of old tennis shoes for just such emergencies . . . bushel baskets of them . . . weren't always mates, ha-ha! . . . but just right to play in. Then he opened a French window onto a terrace and darting through it, told us to come along. The quick deluge had turned into a slow drizzle, an inconvenience we'd more or less learned to disregard. We followed along, Mother and Father, Emily and I, Mrs. Sanger and the Great Educationalist. Bungy, Poodles and Face bore the bushel baskets of tennis shoes as if they had been the pick of a bumper crop of prize clingstones. We went down through the garden and past several enchanting little thatched huts. "Recreation huts during the War!" Mr. Wells called out as we passed. "Furbished them up a bit and set them here. Don't know now and didn't then what for."

We reached a barnlike structure, the inside of which was fixed up with nets, racquets and other evidences of activity. This was obviously Mr. Wells' *Rumpus Room*. He pottered about, tossing tennis shoes around, tightening a thin and quite high little net and getting out a large rubber ball. Thinking that perhaps the young men could take our place we suggested that as there were already so many people, maybe it would be better if we just sat and watched. But Mr. Wells wouldn't hear of it. One of the special beauties of the Wells Game, he said, was that it could be played by any number at a time, and would we please hurry and get into our shoes? With sinking hearts we kicked off our pumps. I recall now with a sick shudder that I had a hole in my stocking through which my large toe was peering. Catching sight of it, I concealed it as best I could by standing on it with the other foot.

Mournfully Emily and I pawed over the piles of tennis shoes, trying to find a pair that would fit. With all due modesty I may say that we both happen to have unusually small feet. All the shoes were men's sizes. Mrs. Wells hadn't bothered to collect any women's. Eventually we each managed to find some which didn't drop off every time a foot was lifted, although Emily's were so big for her she was apt to step with one heel on the toe of the other, a movement which, in order to regain her balance, precipitated her into a series of little running steps.

Emily took off her dark blue milan and in her trim navy dress she didn't look too odd. Maybe her appearance benefited by comparison with mine. I had arranged my hair, which was long, in such a way that if I took off my hat, it fell down. Under these circumstances I was forced to keep on the red Irene Bordoni number with the drooping cock feather. This being the case, there seemed to be no necessity for taking off those Egyptian urn earrings. The immense white tennis shoes set it all off something lovely.

Mother, who wasn't going to play, had settled herself on a bench along the wall where, amid a good deal of mental and physical discomfort, she could look on. Father, who was told he had to play, meekly took off his shoes and paddled about among the bushel baskets looking for some footgear to his fancy. Mother watched him nervously, as was her wont; and then she began a series of those little cooing sounds which we knew indicated extreme agitation. We couldn't discover what was the cause of it until we happened to look down at Father's feet. My distinguished parent for years had had a theatre valet named William Venus. He was long and cadaverous and resembled anything but his voluptuous namesake. Moreover, he was completely color-blind. For untold seasons he had been in the habit of darning Father's socks, using what the wardrobe mistress could spare him in the way of thread, most of which matched the varicolored costumes of the rest of the troup. Venus, even if color-blind, was handy with a needle and his darning lasted a lifetime. Father had become so used to wearing socks that had been repaired in vivid hues, he never gave them a thought. And there he was, pattering about in a particularly lurid pair that had been darned in vermilion, green, royal purple and blush pink. At this point in the proceedings the Americans were, sartorially, anything but ahead.

After we'd all gotten more or less fitted out, Mr. Wells explained the game, and he did so with the earnestness of a school boy enlightening the rules of cricket to a team of novices. It had to do with a number of people being on each team (five in this case) and swatting the ball with the flat of the hand from one to another until the person nearest the high little net smacked it over the top, after which it went down that team in similar fashion and back over the net. It was somewhat akin to the game in "Mr. Britling." There were any number of rules and side-issues, but he talked so fast we considered ourselves geniuses to catch the main idea, and we let the side-issues go. One point we did gather, however, and that was the rule that one person must never under any circumstances hit the ball twice in the same play. That was a most heinous foul and counted a score for the opposing team. Father, Mrs. Sanger and Emily were on one side, Mr. Wells, the Great Education-alist and I on the other. The remaining places were filled in by the visiting Brownies whose true names we never knew.

Off we started, amid a good deal of activity, the brunt of which was borne by the Brownies and Mr. Wells—the latter dashing wildly about, batting the ball either over that high-flown net or at various ones of us on his side, shout-ing "Hit it! Hit it!" with an intensity that might lead one to believe the honor of Oxford and Cambridge was hanging in the balance. We all tried manfully. The Great Educa-tionalist played the way one would imagine a great edu-cationalist would, which was to avoid with dignity as much participation as possible. Mrs. Sanger wasn't so bad, and I don't believe she was so good either, but at least she was moderately inconspicuous. The remainder of us were awful. Emily might have done better if she hadn't gotten constantly tripped up by herself in those tennis shoes. Father behaved a good deal in the manner of Marcelline, the famous Hippodrome clown whose chief activity was to rush about making all sorts of attempts to be helpful just too late to accomplish anything. He went through a lot of energetic motions when he himself was lamming at the ball and when someone on the other side was hitting it, he kept up the same pantomime. It was all very effective but he seldom achieved a direct wallop. As for me, I never once connected up with the wretched object. I would aim my hand at it and swing with all my might, but the only thing I ever succeeded in hitting was my own shoulder.

Mother, watching from the sidelines in acute chagrin, kept up her cooing noises and a little running fire of apology for us, interspersed with a few agonized exhortations: "Gracious, Mr. Wells! I'm afraid our girls aren't quite . . . Otis, dear love, couldn't you just hit something? . . . You see, Mr. Wells, they're not just used to . . . BABY!!!" (Even the cock feather and the long black earrings didn't deter her from calling me that and it added to my humiliation.) "Do try!" God knows we were all trying.

My day had been a decided failure up to then and I made up my mind I must do something to prove my worth. When confronted by the seemingly impossible, I am prone to summon up imaginary situations of patriotic heroism. The Americans by now were behind not only sartorially; they were giving every evidence that ours was a rapidly disintegrating nation. I felt something must be done to vindicate us and done quickly. The ball was coming my way and Mr. Wells was whooping at me to hit it on over the net. I summoned up all my strength and whispering fiercely to myself, "I'm doing this for Uncle Sam and the Spirit of '76," hauled back my arm like a pitcher in a Big League game, closed my eyes and swung with might and main. This time I hit it and it went straight into the face of the Great Educationalist, who was on my own side and no further from me than a couple of feet. It was the only time during the course of the day his face changed expression, but being a man of great self-discipline he didn't say anything. Mr. Wells, however, did. He jumped up and down and shouted, "It's a foul! It's a foul!" and instead of berating me he turned upon my victim. "You did it! You touched the ball twice!" The Great Educationalist, with a calm logic which under the circumstances seemed almost

Socratic, pointed out the fact that one of the touches had
been in the pardonable act of self-defense, but to Mr.
Wells, that was only a weak excuse. I was too horrified at

what I'd done even to apologize. After going over his face
with his fingers and making certain his features were still
there, the eminent worthy changed places with the Brownie
who was the person furthest away from me, and the game
continued, but not for long. Every stroke that followed

seemed a dull anticlimax. Finally, blessedly, Mr. Wells called a halt to the happy contest. We never did catch the gist of his method of score-keeping. Perhaps he intended it that way, for to everyone's astonishment, despite my act of assault and battery, he announced that our side had won, and nobody questioned him.

We shed our tennis shoes like clowns shedding their false feet and thankfully returned to the comfort of our high heels. I kept as well as I could out of the way of the Great Educationalist who eyed me not with rancor, or even reproach, but with a curious critical absorption as if in me he saw the horrible result of faulty American education and an explanation of the murderous gangster impulse. We went back to the house for tea, in the midst of which sooth-ing repast Mr. Wells jumped up and asked if we weren't going to take snapshots of everybody. Emily had brought along her camera but felt shy about asking people to pose. But Mr. Wells, who seemed almost annoyed that he'd had to bring the subject up himself, told her to go get it and again we were all marched out of the house, this time to the garden, where he arranged us in an effective group about the pool. Then he ran over to Emily and peered in the finder, placed her just so and told her not to move, ran back and sat down with the rest of us, squealed out, "Half a mo'!" got up, put a marker for his place, skipped over to make sure she was still focused on us, ran back and told Emily we were quite ready. By this time Emily, stiff from the rigid position he'd made her hold, was suffering from pins and needles down the arms, and she jiggled the camera quite badly trying to push the shutter. That was by way of seeming a minor calamity to Mr. Wells, but she assured him she still had plenty of film, and although he announced that that was a notorious example of American extravagance, he was happily reassured. Emily managed to get one successful exposure and while it is not a thing of particular beauty, we cherish our copies of it for two reasons. The first is that it is the one snapshot she took that summer in which her thumb didn't figure prominently. The other is that some day someone may recognize the Great Educationalist and be able to enlighten us concerning his identity.

CHAPTER 7

SHORTLY after that we left for France. The family stayed on in England. Mother still had a lot of little errands to do. For one thing, she wanted to have a splinter she'd picked out of an old fence in a meadow at Salisbury made into a cross. It would look like a relic, she said, and nobody would suspect that it wasn't; which really wouldn't be wrong, because the old wood was so lovely it ought to be made into something beautiful and dignified. Then too, there was the association of the sheep, which put one in mind of the Manger and to make it all perfect, there was the charming old hand-wrought nail she had blandly yanked out of the choir-loft in the Cathedral (it was loose and about to come out anyway) and that would be just the proper thing to hang it on. In some quaint out-of-the-way street she had found a quaint out-of-the-way cabinet maker who would make the cross. She could get an ivory Jesus in Paris; they were better there and besides it was a Catholic country. So she and Father waited over in London until the cross was finished and they could join us in Paris for her Jesus.

We were now really setting forth on our own and on that territory known delectably as "the Continent." The prospect at once entranced and overawed Emily to such a degree she thought she'd better get back into her money-bag. In England, which she considered a land of integrity, she had left it off but now she was going "among foreigners

and you couldn't tell." She was to wear it only spasmodi-
cally and on occasions when she felt it to be a necessary
precaution, because now it was more bulky than ever. In
addition to her letter of credit, a book of traveler's checks
and a few fifty franc notes, she had also rammed into it her
passport, some pieces of jewelry which obtruded in nubbly
outline, and two letters. Concerning these last she was very
mysterious. Occasionally she'd get them out and read them
over with a soft far-away expression and it required the
utmost control on my part to refrain from peeking and
asking whom they were from. Years later she confessed
they were from her Aunt Huda and Uncle Lloyd but because I had a beau in America who had been writing to me
(prosaic letters they were, all about baseball, but I pretended they were teeming with passion) she felt she should
impress me.

We planned to go not directly to Paris but to stop off
for a time in Normandy. Emily had been told about a little
seaside town halfway between Dieppe and Fécamp called
St. Valery-en-Caux where a Buffalo suitor of hers, who,
she said, was "awfully continental," used to spend his childhood summers. It was recommended as an enchanting place
and as further evidence of its desirability, was said to have
there a branch of the Alliance Française with excellent
teachers. This strikes me now as being a curious induce-
ment but at that time we still had spells of thinking we'd
be better women if we took an occasional course in something. I knew that my French needed brushing up and
Emily said that hers hadn't grown sufficiently even to brush.
At Les Eboulements she had made a few abortive attempts
at conversing with the natives but like the young man in
"Our Mutual Friend" no words, with the possible exception

of *esker* would come forth. She felt weighted down with subjunctives and was reduced to silence; and for Emily ever to be reduced to silence is a minor tragedy.

We crossed the Channel the longer but less painful way, going from Newhaven to Dieppe, where we would spend a night before going on to St. Valery. The ship was one of those small French vessels known by that wonderful maritime name of *paquebot*. The day was calm and sparkling. The sun gleamed on the water and on the red pompons of the sailors. Dieppe, with its church towers, its snug, deep harbor, the line of summer hotels bordering the wide plage, and the 15th Century château crowning its white cliff, is a charming port of entry into France. It all looked just as it should, and we leaned breathless against the rail of the little steamer as they made her fast to the quai of the old Avant Port. The moment the gangplank was down, a bunch of brigand porters rushed on deck in the manner of a buccaneer boarding party, seized all luggage and hustled us off into the customs. It has always seemed a latter day miracle to me how one finds one's baggage amid the pandemonium of a Gallic landing. But somehow it always turns up and there was our collection safe and intact on the *comptoire* of the *douane*. An inspector with a characteristic bushy moustache, soiled uniform and a medal or two asked us if we had anything *à déclarer* in a tone which implied he hoped to heaven we hadn't, so we hastened to assure him we had *rien*. He opened Emily's innovation valise and was instantly hit on the chest by a large tin of English cigarettes. Emily hastened to tell him they weren't hers. They were a present for her Uncle Frank. He picked it up, examined it solemnly, then with a wink said, "Puisque ça c'est rien, on ne le voit pas!" and without further ado replaced it carefully in the suitcase. Our other pieces he didn't bother to open, possibly because he was afraid of discovering other evidences of our perjury. I let ten francs flutter from my purse. He pocketed it with dignity, put chalk heiroglyphics on all our effects and told us to *passer*. The fact that we had "bribed an official" made us feel very European indeed. One of the brigand porters grabbed our things and mumbled a long rigmarole at Emily, who said, "Mercy, what's he saying?" He was asking if these Mademoiselles were taking the Paris train or staying in Dieppe and if so at which hotel were these Mademoiselles going to descend. I told him and he said *entendu*, to meet him outside, he would get us there in style. His solicitude increased our sense of self-importance and we walked with terrific poise out of the customs house, thinking that he must in all likelihood have gone to engage for us the services of the choicest taxi in the line, a Hispano-Suiza no doubt. After a time he appeared with not a Hispano-Suiza, but a small cart like the one in "The Dog of Flanders." Into this he dumped our trunks and larger suitcases, the remaining pieces he fastened onto himself by means of a stout leather strap. I never saw a human being so burdened. If he'd been a donkey we'd have notified the S.P.C.A. As he loaded himself he explained that it wasn't worth the pain to take a taxi, the hotel was nearby, and one could march there facilely at foot. Without further ado he set forth and we meekly followed. This was hardly the style we'd anticipated. We, who had seen ourselves whipping through the city in a handsome equipage, found ourselves progressing on foot, and high heels, stumbling and lurching over the cobble stones behind a glorified wheelbarrow. It was a much longer trek than our cicerone had led us to believe, and in the heat of the afternoon sun we became disheveled and exhausted. Finally the porter slowed up before the door of the hotel, hauled out our luggage and dumped it at the feet of a concièrge, who seemed slightly surprised at our pedestrian manner of arrival but who smiled and being French assumed that after all, it was our affair. We dived into our purses and between us made up a truly handsome pourboire which we handed to the porter. Past experience made me know what would happen but Emily was unprepared for that sudden stream of injured invective which invariably follows the tipping of a French porter. He claimed that it was not enough, that these Mademoiselles had not acted nicely with him, that for them he had given himself many boredoms (ennuis) and that he had a wife and five little ones, also an ancient mother. Emily, before I could stop her, doled him out five francs, an English penny and an American dime. This mollified him somewhat but he still refused to leave and all the time we were making arrangements for a room hung about muttering names at us. His pet term of abuse was *Espèce de concombre, espèce de concombre!* It's surprising how terrifying it can be to be called a "kind of a cucumber" by a Dieppe porter.

We washed and had dinner, after which, it being still light outside, we went for a walk along the shore. It was a quiet evening; the setting sun gilded the façades of the houses; a few lovers, their arms wrapped round each other, strolled along the promenade, pausing now and again to look at the sunset or to kiss quite frankly and resoundingly. A buxom fisherwoman with a small child at her heels laughed and joked in a harsh voice with a group of rough sailors, but when the child would stray she'd call after it and her tone was suddenly gentle music. On one end of a

bench sat a lad in swimming clothes, sea water still beaded
on his chest, and on the other end a formal gentleman reading *L'Intransigeant* and wearing a long black overcoat and
a pair of pearl grey gloves. Two Sisters of Charity passed,
their white coiffs blowing in the breeze like sails on the harbor. It was very serene and very much France.

St. Valery-en-Caux, we knew, was only some thirty
kilometers distant and before going to our room we enquired of the concièrge the best way of getting there. The
concièrge, who was full of activity and very proud of his
English, said, "Right away I find. Two minute please." He
brought forth a railway guide and we waited not two
"minute" but a good twenty while he thumbed energetically and haphazardly through it. It was one of those great
fat publications which lists the time tables of every line in
Europe. We could never have found our way in it and
obviously the concièrge couldn't either, because at one
point I caught a glimpse of the page he was studying and
it had to do with the Bucharest express. After a good deal
of murmuring and head shaking, he slammed the volume
shut, looked up with an expression of triumph and said,
"It's no good! The railroad guide is no good! It says so
itself on the first page!" which seemed a startling admission
for a railroad guide. I suppose what he meant was that the
book was out of date. We asked him how, then, were we to
get to St. Valery. He went for a time into a state of cogita-
tion, then looked up in the manner of Figaro who has just
hit upon an ingenious plan. We might, he said, go to the
railroad station and make "enquirings." It would not be the
right railroad station because the right railroad station was
closed. What they would tell us there, of course, would
only be what he could tell us now, namely, that in order

to reach St. Valery by rail we'd have to start early in the morning, journey inland to Rouen, spend the day there and then take an evening train back to the coast, which, in view of the fact that St. Valery was only thirty kilometers from Dieppe, would have been like going from New York to Greenwich by way of Harrisburg. The other alternative was, of course, the char-à-banc, very swift, very *commode*, very reasonable—but *hélas!* the char-à-banc service hadn't started yet. After all this we decided we'd better hire a car. The concièrge brightened (I think now he must have had a share in the local garage) and said yes, by all means, that was the solution and he'd have us a *belle voiture* on hand in the morning.

We retired early and went to sleep lulled by the sea washing on round pebbles and soothed by the sweet softness of the air of Normandy. Next morning Emily woke me saying, "Why, forever more!" She was gazing in astonishment at something and when I'd followed her gaze I was astonished too. Framed by our window and right outside it was a workman apparently suspended in mid-air. Catching our startled eye he leaned into the room, smiling blandly, and in a gruff voice begged us not to derange ourselves, he was merely there washing the roof. And indeed he was, for a good hour or so. He was out on the top of a porte-cochère which projected just a foot or so below our window-sill and he scrubbed away at it, alternately singing to himself and poking his head into our room from time to time to tell us what a beautiful day it was, how we must *dépêche* ourselves to see the historic town of Dieppe and why hadn't we rung for breakfast? . . . there was the bell, but there! We were a bit slow locating it, so he stepped in and rang it for us. After that we went right ahead, ordered breakfast and ate it in bed, all the while conversing with the genial roof-washer whenever he put his head in at the window. After her initial shock at such informality, Emily was enchanted with the whole idea. It was a quaint way of breaking down her self-consciousness but it worked, and that was her first conversation in French.

The car, that *belle voiture*, arrived to drive us to St. Valery. We felt uneasy about such extravagance. To be sure, we'd struck a reasonable enough bargain with the driver, the equivalent of ten American dollars, but ten dollars was a lot and to hire a car, even a "beautiful wagon," was to us the sort of spending which came under the "drunken sailor" classification. Instinctively I looked about me for fear Mother might suddenly turn up to see us departing in such costly fashion. I needn't have worried on that score. Once seated, nobody could possibly have seen us. The vehicle was an open touring car which the concièrge for some imaginative reason called a *torpédo*. It was an antiquated Fiat which had lost much of its glory and even more of its accessories, including a trunk rack. Accordingly, our luggage had to be stowed in the passenger space, an inconvenience which in no way perturbed the chauffeur. He told us to get in and sit down. He would all arrange. We would see how it was pretty, the route along the shore; we would see, too, how he would dispose of our baggage, there would not even be an all little small (*un tout petit peu*) of movement, was it not so? It was indeed! After taking a few lesser pieces in the front seat beside him, he proceeded to immure us into the back one. Two trunks, two mammoth suitcases, two of those bass-drum hat boxes and a galaxy of lesser carriers towered from the floor before and partly on either side of us, forming an impregnable barrier in the lee of which we rode to St. Valery. The air was sparkling, a salt breeze blew deliciously off the Channel, freshening our cheeks and whipping up the crown of Emily's tweed hat like a pennant. Occasionally we'd hear the voice of the driver asking us if it was not beautiful, the view, and we'd shout back, "Oui,

n'est-ce pas?" We had to take his word for it. All we ever saw on that brief and extravagant outing, except for a patch of blue sky, was a close-up view of a lot of labels saying S.S. *Empress of France*, "Not wanted in Stateroom" and the like.

Emily's suitor, the continental one from Buffalo who had recommended St. Valery and the Alliance Française, had given us the name of a pension. We had written for rooms and had received one of those polite notes of confirmation French landladies with an eye to economy compose in purple ink on a torn and flimsy piece of lined pad paper.

She hastened to assure us she would have a large room for us *bien commode*, overlooking the *bassin*. She was anticipating our arrival with the pleasure the most vivid and she begged us to be so agreeable as to accept her sentiments the most distinguished. Her distinguished sentiments must have

undergone a rude shock when, after the *torpédo* had halted before her gate, the driver pulled out the last of the luggage and there we were behind it. As for us, we realized we'd stopped but we had no notion our pension was reached until we found ourselves face to face with the proprietress.

Her name, as I recall, was Mme. Corue, and one look at her was enough to make one know she was a proprietress. We were beginning to discover that France was a land where people dressed in keeping with their professions.

Maybe it was due to an innate theatrical sense or maybe it was a subtle form of advertising, but in those colorful days a doctor looked like a doctor, an academician couldn't have been anything else *but*, and an actor or musician was as self-evident as a *grue* of the Boulevards. Mme. Corue, too, wore the perfect *costume de rigueur* of the mistress of a provincial pension—a black bombazine blouse with a high collar edged in Binche lace, a gold watch pinned by a blue enamel fleur-de-lys to a rigidly upholstered bosom and, lest that bulwark gave way, attached for further security to a gold chain which went around her neck. Although it was July, she had on a heavy serge skirt and high lace shoes, a fact that should not have surprised us, for a mere seasonal change in no way affects the appearance of a good orthodox *aubergiste*. Her hair, knotted on top, rose in a tight pompadour off a face which was somewhat florid. She was sweet and kind and evidently more practical than imaginative, for she nodded in understanding approval of the baggage arrangement. Ah, yes, she said, to ward off the sun ... *une bonne idée* ... she would remember that. Doubtless she added this item to her extensive store of household hints and from that time on doled it out as sound advice: "When embarking upon a motor trip in hot weather, pile all the luggage in front and on either side of you. You will thus escape the direct rays of the sun."

We were to lodge in the *annexe*, across the road from the main pension. The *annexe* was the second floor of a beguiling old house which overlooked, or, as the French have it, "gave on" the *bassin*, or inner harbor. The ground floor was taken up by a wine shop and hanging out over it was our room, simple but charming, with blue walls and white furniture, the washstand and all that crockery paraphernalia

which comes under the heading of *lavabo* in an alcove discreetly screened with crisp white curtains tied back with
pale blue bows which Madame said were *quelque chose de
fantaisie*. An open French window was framed with similar
white curtains also adorned with blue bows of fantasy.
Through it we stepped out onto a tiny geranium-trimmed
balcony. Leaning over the railing, one could almost have
touched the masts of fishing smacks coming into the snug
harbor. Their sails were red and yellow and blue and the
men who manned them were the dark men of Normandy
who for generations have trailed their cod nets to Newfoundland and back, those "Toilers of the Sea" whose forbears watched the conquering William set forth for Albion.
The *bassin* was edged by a narrow, cobbled street and bordering that, a jumble of small buildings as varying in age as
in color, and a sprinkling of those modern edifices the
French glorify by the name of villa, with weather-softened
façades of rose, blue, or yellow, jammed in amid ancient
beam and plaster houses. There was a 16th Century gem
with leaded casements and ornately carved beams known as
the Henri IV House, no one knew quite why, but it was
a popular belief, or hope, rather, that the amorous monarch
spent a night of love there. Beyond the *bassin* and the town,
a long *jetée* terminated in the inevitable solitary light-house,
and beyond that shimmered the sea. It was really the beginning of what the British call the Channel and the French
know as the Sleeve. Rising on either side of St. Valery were
great chalk cliffs, twins of the Dover ones, topped with
undulating wheat fields, with poppies to make them gay,
and soaring larks to make them eloquent. And along the
edge of these cliffs went winding paths, worn by the generations of lonely women who, of an evening, after their

work was finished, would pace the high promontories, sometimes knitting a sock or crocheting a bit of lace, their eyes searching the horizon for the sight of a home-coming sail.

The pension was comfortable and spotless, and the food excellent. On the long dining table were huge carafes filled with good Normandy cider, and the atmosphere was warm and convivial. The other pensionnaires were pleasant bour- geois Parisians who for years had come to this little resort for their *vacances*. One family in particular I recall chiefly because of the Gallic charm of the head of it, a broker from the Bourse, who, when we seated ourselves, not without trepidation, at our first meal, put us instantly at ease, laugh- ing and joking and making us feel our mistakes in French were as engaging as Yvonne Printemp's English. He opened up conversation announcing that we'd better know from the start he for one never believed in being serious, that he was the *petit-fils de Rabelais* and I to show off the fact that I knew who Rabelais was, said he must mean the great- great grandson because that gentleman had been dead a long time, to which with a sigh he replied, "Oui, mais je regrette toujours sa mort."

Social life in St. Valery centered about the Casino. This was a gay little frame edifice designed in the 90's by some- one who must have admired the Alhambra but could ap- proximate it only in stucco and golden oak. There was a bar of sorts and a *salle de jeu* where members of the re- spectable summer colony would indulge in a riotous game of *boule*, winning or losing all of 25 francs. *Salle de jeu*, I explained wide-eyed to Emily, meant "gambling-room" and she said, "Oh my!" and looked wide-eyed too. We were dying to go inside some evening but we never dared.

That would have been "fast." But we peeked through the windows during the off hours at the one modest gaming table shrouded for the day with a frayed dust cover and felt we were catching a glimpse of Monte Carlo and the life of sin. There was also a *salle de bal* where every Saturday night was held a dismal little festivity known as a "dancing." At one end of this room on a rickety stage with a spool curtain, a few times a season a third-rate road company put on a variety show or a marked-down production of "Hernani." During the day the Casino generally signified a stretch of boardwalk, perhaps fifty yards in all, bordered by rentable chairs on one side and a glassed-in bandstand on the other. That is, the bandstand was glassed in on every side except that facing the sea, which, for some totally unexplained reason, was left open. Every afternoon a gallant little orchestra played its soul out to the sea, and we sat along the boardwalk outside the glass barrier watching in its conservatory all the pantomime of an orchestra in full bloom, and hearing only now and then a faint strain of music wafted back from the water.

Another source of mild astonishment but high delight was the life-saving station maintained by something known in literal translation as "The Society of Initiative," one of those organizations of France which together with the well-known "Anonymous Society" remains veiled in mystery. This particular manifestation of their initiative was a boat-house set on the shore, fairly far from the water. Peering through the window one could see what looked to be most efficient equipment, a *bateau,* a number of *ceintures* and various *appareils* of *sauvetage.* A runway for the boat-wagon led from the house to a point halfway across the beach, where it gave up going farther as perhaps requiring too much initiative. There were doors at either end, both shut and fastened with enormous padlocks, and nailed to each a printed sign which bore the startling announcement that "In case of extreme emergency the key to this Bureau of Lifesaving may, upon request, be obtained at the house of Monsieur le Maire." We used to conjecture with glee a moving rescue drama in which a solemn delegation of St. Valery's leading citizens attired in morning-coats and silk hats calls formally at the house of Mr. the Mayor and sends in their cards. Mr. the Mayor receives them and offers them a glass of wine which, of course, occasions a throbbing toast to the Nation and the wiping away of a tear or two. Then the spokesman discreetly brings up the question of an individual out there in the water who is annoying everyone, including himself, by being in the process of drowning. If, without too gravely deranging himself, Mr. the Mayor could dispense himself of the key to the door of the Bureau of Lifesaving, it would be a gesture on his part most gracious and estimable. But not at all, not at all, cries Mr. the Mayor, it would make him pleasure, a most vivid pleasure! He produces the key and they all shake hands and felicitate one another. The lifesaver, happy and glowing over this civilized exchange of amenities, strolls back to the beach, twirling the key about his finger.

There proved, after all, to be no Alliance Française in St. Valery, but we had plenty of opportunity for practicing our French, inflicting it on Mme. Corue and the other pensionnaires. Our chief victim, however, was Thérèse. She was our constant companion and the daughter of the wine merchant whose little bistro was directly below our room. Good *jeune fille* that she was, she helped *maman* with the household chores and *papa* with his account books but her free time she devoted to us. She was a darling, about our age, short and round, painstakingly polite and at first a

trifle grave. But when Emily told her that the reason she didn't go uphill very well on a bicycle was because she wasn't very "aquatic," Thérèse lost her gravity and with profuse apologies lay on the grass shrieking with rapture, and from then on there was no strain.

Thérèse had a bicycle and we each rented one. They were neither new nor very good, and one had to master the technique of the brake which worked (and sometimes didn't) by squeezing a single lever attached to the right handle-bar. This released some sort of gadget which clamped down on the front wheel, not gradually slowing up the rotation but stopping it dead still and all but hurtling the rider into a somersault. Heavy, rattly things, they were very difficult to propel. We treated them more like perambulators than conveyances. Indeed I scarcely remember our riding them at all except downhill. But with them we covered miles of that sweet country along the straight white roads, poplar-lined, across tidy fields through which rippled serene, well-behaved streams, past lonely Norman churches with towers square-topped by the cock of Gaul, into little settlements of beam and plaster houses with thatched roofs and gardens bright with roses and small vegetables. Thérèse knew everybody. Sometimes we'd pause at an open kitchen door and while she chatted with the woman of the ménage we'd gaze with pleasure at the huge copper pots burnished and gleaming above the stove, the rows of earthenware spice jars, the bunches of herbs and garlic hanging from the blackened rafters. Our bicycles bumping along beside us, we'd travel the winding cobbled streets of the town where communities of fishermen and their families mended the red nets which stretched sometimes across two and three houses.

We swam every day, or almost every day. Once or twice a slight breeze blew up, making the water moderately rough, in which event there would appear a sign saying that all baths of sea were *defendu* on account of naughty sea (*mer mauvaise*). The sea never stayed naughty for long and we'd go in from the pebbly beach which was agony to our feet. The French bathers weren't bothered by those vicious little stones, possibly because their shoes have in-nured their feet to pain. Our swimming was not much bet-ter than our bicycling. Emily was right about not being very "aquatic." She could swim those fifty strokes she'd talked about on the *Montcalm* if she counted, but if any-one spoke to her she'd lose the rhythm and sink like a plummet. She hugged the shoreline, swimming along it in rather shallow water and putting her foot down every other stroke to make certain the bottom was still there. Thérèse and I, on the other hand, plunged brave as seals into the chilly depths of the Sleeve and tried, at least I did, to look as if we were heading straight for England. Thérèse was an expert swimmer, but Emily said that watching me in-spired not so much admiration as a desire to call on the Mayor and secure that key to the Bureau of Lifesaving. I was always able to swim indefinitely (provided the water is calm) but only if I used my own peculiar stroke. This started out as a breast stroke and ended up in a movement like a plunging submarine. What fascinated Emily was not so much my breast stroke as my perpendicular method of doing it. Practically upright, I'd rise well above the water and then sink below its surface, like a California oil well in action. However, I covered great distances with slow regularity, and my endurance was phenomenal. Long after Emily had completed her fifty strokes and subsequent bob-bings and paddlings in a half sitting position (another of her aquatic activities) I'd just be coming in, in majestic surge and retreat.

We were in St. Valery for the 14th of July. The expression of patriotic sentiment began at dawn when a cannon directly below our window went off with a report which almost blew us out of bed. It made any American giant cracker sound like a BB gun. For a moment we thought the war had started again and that Big Bertha was trained on our house. But the *femme de chambre* enlightened us. She was bringing in our *café au lait* just as the thing went off again and it never occurred to her to bat an eye, let alone drop the tray. It was just *une petit cérémonie* she said, *pour saluer la Bastille.* That '75 continued saluting the Bastille at five and ten minute intervals all morning and Emily and I, who both hate explosions to a psychopathic degree, retired to a distant wheat field until the Bastille apparently considered itself sufficiently saluted.

That evening on the quai they had *feux d'artifice* and "fires of artifice" was so much more what they really were like than "fire-works." With Gallic economy, rockets were released one at a time and after long intermissions. They weren't very good rockets but each received a round of applause and people gazing with wonder said *A-a-a-a-h! Que c'est beau!* Most of the rockets were aimed in the general direction of the sea, but the national trait of individualism manifested itself in one which went hissing like a flaming snake amid the crowd who screamed and cried *Attention! Attention!* then when they'd made sure nobody had been blown to bits, laughed merrily and applauded that too.

Following the "fires of artifice" came dancing in the street to the music of the village band composed of local musicians each of whom had a different conception of the tune. But the effect was gay and everybody danced,—

fisherfolk, shopkeepers, summer trippers and one formal individual in a Prince Albert and top hat who was un-
doubtedly Mr. the Mayor, out to prove that while the
democracy of the Republic was not to be questioned, *ces
Messieurs* of official life must maintain their dignity. We
danced along with the rest of them. Our partners to begin
with were the nice bourgeois gents from the pension, but
little by little we found ourselves whirling about with the
villagers—friends of Thérèse, or shopkeepers with whom
we'd talked. Then at one moment I was unexpectedly seized
by an unknown elderly gentleman with a beard and felt
hat. I guess he had on more than that but that was all I
noticed. For a time we pivoted solemnly about the square,
not exchanging a word. I was too shy and he was obviously
too dignified. At the same time a sailor swept Emily off
into a lively jig and they too said nothing except when their
gyrations drew them closer and closer to the water's edge
when Emily would come out with an occasional "Oh
mercy!" After that we danced with everybody, just as
everybody else was doing. It was a complete expression of
heartwarming gaiety and that they should have taken us in
and allowed us to be a part of it gave us at once a feeling
of intoxicating joy and humility. Around and around the
place on the *bassin* we danced, and the broken reflection
of lights danced also on the water, while the little boats
bobbed up and down in time to the music.

We saw a lovely gay young girl of about sixteen, with
black hair, wide brown eyes and dark skin which had a
warm glow, as if the color in her cheeks never quite came
to the surface. She wore a cape which swathed her lithe
body, and she danced with one young man after another,
the young men with their arms about her waist and she not

holding them at all but moving lightly and gracefully in perfect time with them and the music. There was a moment when just as she swayed past us a gust of wind blew aside her cape. She had no forearms at all, but two tiny fingers at the ends of the stumps where her elbows should have been. We must, involuntarily, have started at the sickening and pitiful sight, for a ghoulish old woman who had been watching us came up and pointed her out as one of the local sights of interest. She had been "marked," the old crone said, because her mother had opened the door to an armless peddler three months before the little one was born, and at the shock had fainted dead away. All the village knew then that the baby would be marked and it was so. The music finally stopped and the crowd dispersed, some couples continued to dance their way home, others formed lines of four and six and skipped through the narrow streets singing. The genial man from the Bourse took Emily by one arm and me by the other and calling to his wife and *gosse* to join along, marched us all back to the pension whistling alternately "La Madelon" and "Yes, We Have no Bananas." Exhilarated but exhausted, we plopped into bed and that cannon might have saluted the Bastille all night. We would never have heard it.

Next day we visited the church. I forget now its name, but I remember it was dedicated to La Vierge Marie, and before her altar, a touching assortment of offerings, some dating from days past, some freshly recent. One of these caught our eye immediately, and we knew it must be the offering of the parents of the lovely armless girl. It was in wax, a pair of tiny hands sculptured with such artistry, such tenderness and pity, one wanted to weep. They hung suspended by a twisted scarlet cord before the serene statue of the Virgin, and they moved timidly in the air as if in endless supplication. I wonder still who the artist could have been. Ship models, too, had been placed there. Some were in payment of a vow made when a ship had been nearly lost in a tempest, some waited there in prayer for those who had set forth gaily with the fishing fleet but had not returned. It was all so simple, so trusting and intimate. We felt we were trespassing and we tip-toed out, leaving the little offerings to their silent communion with the compassionate Lady of the Sea.

We might have stayed on in St. Valery for months, but we'd planned to go to Paris, and one day we announced firmly that we'd be departing the next, because if we didn't, we knew we'd never get away. That evening we had a party for Mme. Corue, Thérèse and all the guests of the pension. We had bought presents for everyone, cheap awful things like souvenir shell-frames or children's sand toys, intended as humor. With each present went a limerick, in French, and over that effort we'd slaved as for a Ph.D. The limerick is a verse-form unknown to the children of Ronsard and Victor Hugo, and the bewildered recipients of ours neither laughed nor comprehended one word of them. Moreover the fact that we'd lavished a useless present on everybody for no apparent reason merely confirmed their suspicion of our lack of mental stability, the mad extravagance of all Americans, and a firmer resolve never to pay the National Debt. However, Madame smiled and said we were *des rigolos*, which was the equivalent of saying we meant well . . . and she was quite right, we did.

CHAPTER 8

THE railway which bore us from St. Valery was the "Chemin de Fer de la Manche" which we never called by any name other than "The Road of Iron of the Sleeve." It's a picturesque line and our second class carriage looked like one of those early American coaches which used to be on exhibition in the Grand Central Station. The one daily train winds its way in leisurely fashion through the Normandy countryside, stopping at every village and crossroads and occasionally in the middle of a wheat field for no apparent reason, unless perhaps the engineer takes a sudden fancy to pick a few poppies. At Rouen it gives up, the gallant little engine is detached (doubtless after being duly congratulated) and the cars are coupled onto a less colorful, through line to Paris. We decided to break the trip and enlarge our cultural vista by stopping off in Rouen for the night, and why our experience in that historic town didn't leave its mark on the rest of our lives is proof positive that there must be a special Providence set apart to watch the faltering steps of such ninnies as we. However, we got through the day before that action of Providence was needed.

We checked our luggage at the station and with Baedekers in hand, open like hymn books, went on foot about that lovely ancient city. For the first time we realized that now at last we were "abroad." London had been exciting, but somehow one feels its antiquity only at special points of pilgrimage such as the Tower, Westminster Cloisters, or the Inner Temple, to find which one journeys through busy thoroughfares on a prosaic bus. Even amid the tidy loveliness of Salisbury, or the carefully maintained splendor of Hampton Court, one hasn't that sense of being transported into another world and another century. We took the first narrow winding street, and almost at once found ourselves in the Place de l'Hôtel de Ville. It and that other Gothic gem, the church of St. Ouen, rose before us. On either side little shops nestled under the overhanging eaves of ancient buildings, as they must have in the days of the Guilds. A peasant in a black smock and sabots pushed along a cart loaded with exquisitely arranged cabbages, and a scissors grinder made known his presence in a weird unintelligible cry which might have been in the language of the Norman Dukes. The sky was flecked with small, attenuated clouds, and in the soft air, to brand the scene as being French, was that distant scent of open sewage which, curiously enough, one comes in time to like. Suddenly, miraculously we were in the Middle Ages, or rather, *le Moyen Age*. Past the Palais de Justice and down the rue Jeanne d'Arc, under the Tower which also bears her name, where her pitiful trial took place, and then at last we were in the old Market Place, standing on the spot where that guileless girl from Domremy was burned to death. It was Emily's first experience of the sort. She stood in the center of that beautiful and heartbreaking square murmuring, "This is the place. This is the very place." And quietly, unpremeditatively, we both stooped down and touched the cobblestones. We were moved to the point of wanting to burst into loud sobbing. For all our conscientious sight-seeing there had, up to now, been a certain deliberately planned quality to our appreciation. Our response to things, while enthusiastic, had been anything but hyper-sensitive. But we responded now to Joan of Arc, a girl of our own age. We responded with all the warmth and ache of our young hearts. This was what we'd come abroad for, this breathless moment, when we put down our hands to touch the spot where a momentous and agonizing hour of history had passed.

We wandered on down the rue de la Grosse Horloge and on to where the little thirteenth century houses nestle, as if for sanctuary, about the great Cathedral. We lifted our eyes to the flamboyant façade, and then up and up and ever up, following the soaring line of that "tallest finger toward heaven," the *Tour de Beurre*, and something inside us was stirring too profoundly for us to express except in simple phrases. Emily with a catch in her breath said gently, "You know, back in Indiana there's a lovely phrase of yearning. People say, 'I hope I get to go.' Well, I've gotten to go, and here I am, standing in front of the Cathedral in Rouen, France . . . Europe!"

We went up the steps and through the door, and the vast nave unrolled almost audibly before us, and all along in the dark side-chapels were the wavering lights of tapers as tremulous as ourselves. Near the holy water font sat a black-hooded nun. Her face was pallid and as long drawn out as those of the carved saints in their narrow niches, and she kept repeating in a low, harsh whisper, "Pour les pauvres, Mesdames, pour les pauvres!" I bought a candle from her and although I didn't know much about such ceremonies, I placed it on a little spike beside the others which flickered before the shrine of Joan. She hadn't been canonized for very long and it was sweet to think of her coming into the eminent name of St. Joan. For all my Universalist forbears I went down on my knees to thank her and France and God for letting me be there. It was only after a little while that I felt suddenly self-conscious and got to my feet, looking about to see if anyone had noticed me. But the only person I saw was Emily, who on the opposite side of the shrine was also getting to her feet. She, too, had put a candle there and had said her prayer. Without a word we went on together toward the Lady Chapel.

Halfway up the nave we were accosted by an old harpy who was sitting behind a table of lighted tapers. She called out something to us and when we paid no attention, left her place, ran after us and started clutching at our sleeves. She was pointing at the small postern door opening onto the spiral stairway to the belfry. We must climb up to the top, she said. Why we felt it incumbent upon us to obey her, is as incomprehensible as why we felt obliged to tip her 50 centimes for issuing this unpleasant order. Emily and I both detest heights to such a degree that even climbing a step-ladder makes us sick at our stomachs, but we let ourselves get pushed and shrilled into that Stygian tunnel. The door slammed to behind us and there was no alternative but to climb. Up the worn stone steps we trudged in pitch darkness except at infrequent moments when a slit of light from a mullioned window revealed the nasty fact that we were leaving *terra firma* further and further below us. Up and up we wound our panting way and yet we seemed to be getting nowhere. Round and round like slow-motion squirrels in an elongated cage. It began to take on a quality of nightmare and we each suffered an attack of that paralyzing childhood phobia, the feeling that we were being chased

from behind by "something awful." Even as a grown
woman when I find myself in the dark, I have an unfortunate tendency to think up all sorts of Poe-like horrors. I
don't believe in ghosts but I become suddenly afraid of
them, and a myriad of old wives' superstitions cross my
mind. How I'd derived the notion I can't imagine, but at
that point I heard myself telling Emily that if cathedral
bells started ringing while you were in the belfry, the
vibrations would drive you mad. Emily, who in addition
to her other terrors was undergoing an acute spell of
claustrophobia, collapsed onto the step she was treading
and managed to croak, "Is it time for the bells to ring?"

"How should I know when the bells ring?" I snapped.

"What about the Angelus?" Emily said. "You know,
that painting."

Fear, I concluded, had caused her to take momentary
leave of her senses and I asked her what the heck a painting had to do with it.

"They heard bells, didn't they, those peasants? And
Millet was French; he must have known when French bells
ring. It was the end of the day in that picture and it's the
end of the day now. Unless . . ." she added with a note
of hysteria, "we've been climbing all night and are starting
out on tomorrow."

I could offer nothing more helpful than the information
that back home in Bryn Mawr the angelus used to ring at
six. Emily asked was it six now and I said I didn't know,
because by the dim light from one of those window slits it
was apparent my watch had stopped. Emily said, well, hers
was going but it was in her safety-pocket, and pulling up
her skirt, she started frantically plunging into her over-
stuffed sporran. In the midst of this activity there suddenly

caught up with us a group of five or six other tourists, poor
yokels like us, trapped by the crone two or three miles below. They didn't look any too happy, either.

Their presence eased our panic and Emily came hastily
back out of her money belt. "Keep close to them," she
hissed. "There'll be less danger of going mad if the bells
ring."

"What makes you think so?" I said.

"There'll be more of us together," she said. "That will
make it harder for the vibrations to concentrate." This was
an example of Emily's reasoning at its best, but it seemed
rather reassuring at the time. We followed along with the
others and in a minute or two were laughing and skipping
our way to the top.

We came out into fresh air and a dazzling sunset. I guess
there must have been a magnificent view too but we didn't
dare look. However, we gazed with delight at the sky and
some charming carvings in the balustrade and felt so relieved to be again in the open, we never noticed when the
other pilgrims left. Suddenly we were aware that they'd
gone and we were alone on the summit of that great cathedral. Then, as if twenty minutes previously we hadn't
worked ourselves up into a sufficient wax, we began, in a
spirit of fun and fantasy, a little series of supposings. What
if, one of us suggested, we were up here at the top and no
one else had come. The bells had not made us mad because we were outdoors when they rang. But we were
alone . . . nobody knew we were up there. Even the old
crone had gone home. The situation offered endless possi-
bilities and, inspired by the fascination of horror, we went
on elaborating. Suppose, for instance, in the confusion of
turrets, buttresses and pinnacles we couldn't find the door

to the stairway or, having found it, suppose it proved to be locked? In such an event we'd call loudly but who could hear us at that height? We waved and wig-wagged but no-

body saw us. It was growing dark and eventually we were forced to spend the night huddled against a cornice. Next day, we went on to say, was a holiday and the door remained locked. Again we waved our handkerchiefs, and again to no avail, so we started taking off our clothes and signaling with them but still the passers-by in the street far,

far below never looked up. Then, we conjectured (and by now the tale had taken on a ghoulish reality), we dropped our garments piece by piece down over the edge, hoping someone would investigate whence they were falling. But there was a strong breeze blowing and most of them caught in transit on gargoyles and projecting bits of masonry, and still nobody noticed. We became crazed with fright and hunger. There remained nothing for us to do but step forth onto that dizzy parapet, closing our eyes and clinging frantically to one another and a fragile stone pinnacle. And there we stood, stark naked in the wind and weather. For a time nothing happened, and then from far down below we heard a murmur of voices which swelled into a mighty roar. We didn't dare open our eyes, much less let go of the pinnacle in order to wave. We just stood there motionless, trusting that curiosity would force some of the populace to come up. We would be shamed, even possibly arrested, but we'd be saved. But not a soul ever came up! Word went round that a miracle had come to pass and that we were holy manifestations. The bishop declared the view of us from the square below a point of pilgrimage, and as further expression of reverence, ordered the passage-way to the belfry locked and barred, for no human must ever profane the spot where we stood. We died there, of course.

What we actually did was to scare ourselves so with this little flight of fancy, we shot back into the tunnel like rabbits to their warren, clattered down the spiral stairway and catapulted through the door and on past the old troll so fast we blew out her tapers.

We were exhausted after this, so we returned to the station, extracted our over-night bags from the check room, and, footsore and weary, plodded to the place where we planned to spend the night. I wonder now what gave us such endurance. But we felt it would not have been in keeping with the surrounding atmosphere of antiquity to have taken a taxi. If we had, it is doubtful if the driver, provided he were a God-fearing family man, would have abandoned us at that address.

We had acquired the address through my mother. Mother was a joiner. She would join any organization of which her friends were presidents or committee members, provided, of course, the dues weren't excessive. Once having joined, she seldom did much about her affiliations, and dear knows never dreamt of going to any meetings, but she kept on joining others because, she'd explain, she thought they might prove useful sometime and besides such nice women belonged to them. One of her enthusiasms was an instructive little endeavor known as "The Ladies' Rest Tour Association." Its purpose was to provide lists of comfortable but inexpensive and, of course, highly respectable lodgings for ladies traveling alone and unprotected through Europe. It publishes a monthly pamphlet which contained sprightly articles penned by certain of the itinerant members, telling about the cosy inn one of them had found in Avignon, recommending a highly intellectual pension in Perugia, or putting fellow travelers on the trail of a Swiss tea room where the coffee was "just like home." There was also issued a general European lodging list for the use of members only, they being supposedly on their honor not to pass the information along to any outsider (one of the aims of the society was to "keep Europe unspoiled"). Mother had culled the address of a

Rouen boarding house out of this invaluable pamphlet and had sent it to us. She may have written it down wrong, or the Ladies' Rest Tour publication may have been guilty of a misprint, but it was clear someone had blundered, for the hostelry proved to be one which had very little to do with "rest" and Lord knows nothing remotely to do with "ladies." As surely as we were what our mothers would have called "nincompoops," that house was one which our mothers also would have called "of ill repute."

We rang the bell and after a time the door was opened a crack by a frowsy maid who didn't seem to want to let us in. But we smiled and said, *Bon soir* and blandly asked to see *La Madame* (meaning "landlady"). The maid looked slightly astonished and walked off, returning in a second with the landlady, who looked even more astonished. She was awfully dressy and luridly made up, hardly the type one would associate with the Ladies' Rest Tour and the elderly New England gentlewomen who supported it. We told her we'd like a room for the night, a seemingly simple demand but one which obviously increased her astonishment, for she stepped back in a blank manner and gave no reply. I was afraid she thought that two girls arriving alone and on foot might detract from the gentility of her pension, so, to establish our respectability, I told her that her house had been recommended to us as just the place for *deux jeunes filles*. She murmured a faint *Ah?* and beckoning us to follow, led us down a hall. It was lined on either side with smallish rooms, rather elaborately decorated. Some of the doors were open, and we caught glimpses of the other guests who seemed quite surprised to see us and we were indeed surprised to see them. They all appeared to be young women in very striking evening dresses. This was certainly unusual, but we concluded they must all be waiting to go out to a dinner-party. It never once occurred to us that we weren't exactly in keeping with the *ton* of the place, I, in

my Buster Brown panama and Emily in her pepper and salt tweeds.

Madame led us up several flights of stairs and allotted us a modest room quite removed from the more elaborate ones below. She explained we'd be more *tranquille* there. Then, in a faint, far-away voice, she asked how we'd happened to come to her place. We told her we'd read all about it in a book published by an American society. She hadn't said much up to now, but this item of information caused her to lose all power of articulation, for she opened and closed her mouth several times but nothing came forth. Finally, with a wan, Camille-like wave of the hand, she backed out of the room and closed the door. Her behavior had been very odd, but with our faith in the Ladies' Rest Tour ever bright, we dismissed her as being a "character."

We washed, went out and found a quiet near-by restaurant where we dined. We were less shy about going into restaurants than we'd been in London, possibly because there were no other places in which to eat. Then we returned to our snug abode. The frowsy maid, still looking astonished, admitted us, and we went down the long hall, tiptoeing because the doors were all closed now, and we didn't want to disturb anybody. We could hear the sound of laughter and music coming from a back room but we felt too tired to join in the fun, so we climbed the flights of stairs and went to bed. We were very comfortable but I couldn't help thinking that this was an eccentric sort of pension, and Emily remarked that it lacked that "homey" quality of the one in St. Valery.

Once in the night we woke with a start. People were walking in the corridor outside, we could hear a man's voice and someone tried the handle of our door. Then we heard Madame speaking sharply to whoever it was and evidently she pulled him away. We thought it very nice and motherly of her to be up watching out for her boarders, but just in case we might be disturbed again we did take the precaution of pushing the bureau against the door. After which we slept the sleep of babes.

The following morning, bright and eager as daisies, we rose, packed and asked for the bill. Madame told us it was not her custom to make out a formal account but she named a sum which was most reasonable, and as we paid it we told her what a pleasant sojourn we had had there and how we'd most assuredly recommend her establishment to all our friends. Her eyes glazed over a bit at that, and faintly she asked us if we'd have the *bonté* to give her the name of the American *Société* which had informed us about her. She would like, she said, to write to them. We gave her the name and address of the Ladies' Rest Tour Association, and left her to start what, we trust, proved to be an interesting and illuminating correspondence.

At the station we waited a considerable time for the Paris train. We always waited an interminable time for trains. I guess that was my fault. I can't control my mania for getting to stations way ahead of schedule. I confess to this failing only because Emily, who is co-author, insists that I do. (She, incidentally, likes to arrive just in time to swing aboard the observation car as it whizzes by.) In those days I was even worse. Emily used to say that the moment I discovered the hour for a train departure, I reacted the way a hunter in India must when he comes across fresh tiger tracks. He rushes home with the thrilling news of his discovery and starts laying plans. He packs his provisions, gets his equipment in order, makes calculations regarding the weather and sets forth to a snug look-out. There he lies in wait for a night or two until his tiger happens along. This, she vowed, was my normal behavior when lying in wait for a train. Therefore, at Rouen, we went to the station after breakfast and had a very nice early lunch there later on. After that I decided it was about time for us to go out on the platform in order, to continue Emily's unfortunate metaphor, to be within closer range when our train should come prowling up to its water-hole. It was a judgment on her that at this point she all but lost the means of continuing any further her European trip.

The Cathedral was just visible above the distant rooftops. Emily, standing on tiptoe at the edge of the platform, pointed at the *Tour de Beurre* in an exalted and lofty gesture. This was a moment to remember, she said, we must try to fix it in our memories. We didn't have to try very hard. Her pocket book was a grey suède "envelope" fastened, not too securely, with a blue enamel clasp. It had a strap across the back through which to slip one's hand, a detail which was considered particularly smart. Shallow and not very large, the thing was intended to hold only a few bare necessities. But that day Emily had rammed it to bursting point. It was replete with coin purse, comb, cigarette case, wads of postcards, a Roger and Gallet pomade lipstick and one of those compacts which came in a small cardboard box with a tiny puff and powder in cake form known as a "Dorine." In addition to all this, she had transferred to it the entire contents of her money-belt—passport, traveler's checks, jewelry, even those much thumbed letters from Aunt Huda and Uncle Lloyd; because, she said, going to Paris and all, you couldn't tell what you might be asked for. At the moment of her skyward gesture her hand was through the strap and the purse was upside-down. Gazing at the distant spire she was saying, "You know, it's so lovely, I feel as if something were about to burst," and those were the truest words she ever uttered, because something did. It was the chic enamel clasp, and her purse opened out wide in the manner of a steam shovel. The contents clattered down with the rush of a rock-slide and disappeared from view. For a moment we stood there, stunned by the cataclysm, then we both squatted at the edge of the platform and peered down at the tracks a good distance below. There they were. All of Emily's possessions scattered along ten feet of the road-bed. Her letter of credit in transit had opened out, money and coins were strewn over the stones like oats in a plowed field, her Roger and Gallet pomade was wedged between two spikes, even her "Dorine" had fallen to pieces and the puff was resting jauntily on a gleaming rail. I straightened up just in time to jerk her back as a train roared in past her nose and on top of all her possessions. At that precise instant, the Paris train, the one we'd been stalking for five or six hours, sneaked in behind us on the other side of the platform. Our porters, to whom Emily had been referring as our "beaters," galloped up to arm themselves with our baggage and to tell us we must despatch ourselves as the train waited only a few minutes.

We told them what had happened and they in turn bellowed the information to one another and the fast collecting crowd. Other travelers hurried up, waiters dashed forth from the station restaurant, even the ticket agent ran out anxious to get in on the news first hand. We pointed, and the porters gesticulated energetically at the collection of Emily's worldly goods strewn below the railway carriage. Then everyone began to offer advice. One could, they said, back up the train, but someone else objected that the mail was being unloaded and such *mouvement* would derange the postal agents, to say nothing of the

objects of this lady. Someone else made the helpful remark that she might salvage what was left of her little
numbers after the train had gone which, *évidemment*,
would be some fifteen minutes after the hour of departure
of the Paris train. A waiter put in the gallant suggestion
that if the gravity of the situation were made sufficiently
clear, the Paris train might wait. But the ticket agent
shouted in righteous indignation that the Paris train had
never waited for anyone except M. Poincaré and the waiter
was an imbecile. No, there was nothing for us to do but
wait there until the train had gone, the train which was
not the Paris train, for example; then the lost objects could
be salvaged unless already ruined, *bien entendu*, by the
passage of the train, that one, in effect, which was not the
Paris train, of course, is it not? In that case even the young
lady's passport would no longer be of any use and she
would have forfeited her right to remain in the country;
or, came the note of cold native logic, to leave it. This was
a fine point for debate, one after their own hearts, and they
were just settling down with fervor for an all-day discus-
sion when a voice like a fog horn resounded above the bed-
lam. "Me voici!" it roared and it came from below the platform. Peering down the narrow gap between it and the
train we located its owner, a burly workman, his baby blue
smock billowing out around him, stretched out flat on his
stomach between the wheels. He was gathering in Emily's
possessions, passport, money, letter of credit, even the
Roger and Gallet pomade and the scattered parts of her
"Dorine." Everyone watched and spurred him on with
heartening suggestions, and he himself held forth in an ora-
tion upon his own audacity, ingenuity and general good
sense. By some miracle the Paris train waited. Perhaps there

was an extra amount of baggage that day. Certainly no one
made any attempt to hold it. I myself think it waited because the engineer was hanging out the cab window watching and didn't want to miss anything.

The workman backed out from between the wheels,
which mercifully remained stationary, trotted around the
engine, up some steps at the far end of the platform and
ran to us triumphant, his hands and pockets full of Emily's
little treasures. The crowd, with murmurs of admiration
and relief, hustled us over to the Paris train. Emily, grateful
to the verge of tears, kept spluttering hybrid phrases of the
"Merci *ever* so much" variety, pressing more and more
money into the kindly, outstretched hand. He assured us
such exertion was nothing for such a man as he and that
he loved America. He had never been there but he knew
well "Charlot" Chaplin and Gloria "Svanson." However,
in all honesty he must confess that he had not been able
to retrieve quite all. Down there, lying in a particularly
dangerous spot, was a fifty franc note. It was reposing itself
between the wheels and any minute now the train would
be leaving. He could not, even for America, risk his life
further. He had to think of his family and to invite any
more danger would be unreasonable. Emily, frankly weep-
ing by now, agreed that indeed he had already dared too
much, and pressed more money into his liberal hand, this
time for his family. He thanked her and bowed and said
he must now return to work. A humble artisan, we told
each other, who had done such a magnificent thing with
no thought of himself. It made us feel noble and warm.
Our train started to move, we yanked loose the window
strap and leaned out for one last look. There under the

other train which was placidly taking on water and would not leave for another half hour, was our hero workman. He was just backing out from between the wheels and as we passed, he stood up and waved good-bye with the fifty franc note in his hand.

CHAPTER 9

OUR train bustled along fussily and at alarming speed. Every hundred yards its whistle let out a high nervous shriek to the countryside at large. "Why, it's saying Bo-Peep!" Emily exclaimed. "And look— There's a Bo-Peep!" She was pointing at a signal man who had come out of his shack. In one hand he held a tall staff, for all the world like a shepherd's crook, except that it said *arrêt* on top; with his other hand he led by a long rope a large family of goats, which he had lined up across the road in lieu of a gate. He gave us a dignified flourish of his crook as we shrilled past.

The farther we journeyed toward Paris, the faster the train went, like a horse smelling its oats. Ours was the end car and the engineer rounded all corners as if he were playing "Crack-the-whip." Emily decided she wouldn't look out the window because she'd just as soon not know when we left the rails.

I suggested we improve the time and our minds by making out vocabulary lists. Emily says that in those days I used to have spells of being revoltingly academic and that if her tendency to quote Homer annoyed me, she was equally irritated by my sudden attacks of mental uplift. Her French vocabulary was sadly abridged and I told her, quite pedantically, that the way to master a language was to learn fifteen or twenty new words a day. We should write out lists, I said, which we could paste on the mirror to memorize every morning while brushing the teeth or hair. It was a simple and painless method and she might as well start in now. For some reason she complied with surprising meekness. I guess the purse-bursting episode had cowed her somewhat. I unpacked our one dictionary and a volume of Proust with which I was struggling. Proust has always bored me profoundly but I thought to be seen reading "Du Coté de chez Swann" lent me intellectual tone. I offered Emily my "Hundred Best Poems of the French Language" but she said no, she preferred to look about at the signs and things and pick out more useful words. By the end of an hour she announced proudly that she knew how to say "lean out," "brake," "No Smoking," "safety-valve," "spit," and "water-tap." "There! I hope you're satisfied!" and her tone was acid. "That ought to make me a source of wit and charm to all the French people I meet."

In my preoccupation, I hadn't looked out the window, and when I did there was little to see beyond the usual suburban houses of hideous *moderne* architecture. But something caught my eye, and I looked again. It was that amazing piece of construction which suddenly straddles over the horizon and rises up into the air like a colossal Daddy-Long-Legs, a sight which never fails to make my throat contract.

"Look!" I said.

Emily, absorbed by the word for "Fire Extinguisher," glanced out and said, "Yes. The cable tower of a cantilever bridge." The Kimbroughs of Indiana build bridges and she was prone to toss off a technical term now and then for effect. Not that she knew what she was talking about, her only knowledge of bridge-building having been based on helping her little brother with his Meccano. Then she looked again.

"It seems awfully high for any bridge," she said. "Must be some sort of tower. A tower!" She grabbed my arm and pointed, unable to make a sound. And I said, "Yes, that's it!"

"The Eiffel Tower!" she whispered. "The Eiffel Tower is in Paris, France! The Louvre is there and Notre Dame and Napoleon's Tomb, but not me!" But Emily Kimbrough, born way off in Muncie, Indiana, and Cornelia Skinner, whose forbears came from Vermont and Missouri, were actually getting there.

The usual things happened to us at the Gare St. Lazare, where the inevitable band of maniacal porters seized our pieces of luggage, flung them on the platform a number of times to see if they'd bounce, hurtled us across the station and began demanding more money before we'd even tipped them. Eventually we came to rest in an open taxi. Our interval of rest, however, was the negligible span of time between the slamming of the door and a convulsion in low gear. After that, the possibility of survival was anybody's guess—not that anybody was interested enough to guess.

The taxi was one of those venerable vehicles which had doubtless rushed troops to the front in August, 1914, and was still rushing. It rattled and sputtered and progressed in the manner of a fleeing kangaroo. The driver never stopped talking. We could see the ends of his moustache working furiously the entire way. Occasionally he'd bellow greetings or anathema to other drivers; the rest of the time he addressed himself to the view, the gear-shift or himself at the top of his lungs. He drove in traditional manner and at horrifying pace. His only concession to crossings was to sound his horn, and putting on greater speed, rush at them as if leading a cavalry charge. Every other driver was doing exactly the same thing. Each blasted his horn at every intersection, and kept on blasting it all the way down the block as a warning that he was coming to the next intersec-

tion. As it was impossible to distinguish one warning note above another, the idea was a bit confused but the general volume was magnificent.

Now and then a solitary gendarme waved at the traffic with a white stick which looked like a diploma. Sometimes one of them would blow a whistle barely audible above the din, but nobody paid the slightest attention.

Down the Boulevard Haussmann we whizzed, catapulted across the Place de l'Opéra but didn't take it in because at that moment our eyes were tight shut, shot down the rue de la Paix and careened giddily around the Vendôme column. Another taxi was careening with us, neck to neck. It, too, was open and a girl sat in the back.

"Why, forever more!" Emily cried. "There goes Agatha Clark!" She hoisted herself into a precarious kneeling position and leaning over the swaying side shouted, "Agatha! Agatha, darling!"

The young woman stared for a moment, then she, too, rose and waved, and as our taxi roared ahead of hers, called out, "Rumpelmayer's. Tomorrow at four-thirty. Tea."

"And who may Agatha Clark be?" I enquired, somewhat irked that Emily should rate a social engagement the moment she got to Paris. Agatha, it seems, was someone with whom Emily had attended Miss Wright's school. She had been several classes ahead of her, and Emily hardly knew her at all, but to come across an acquaintance struck her as being peculiarly wonderful.

This was the sort of thing which made Paris so gay, she said, and added it might be a good idea to buy an engagement pad. She did meet Agatha at Rumpelmayer's next day and for five minutes they didn't stop talking. After that, they couldn't think of anything more to say to one another, and they have never met since. But at the time, to "meet up" with a fellow American on "The Continent" seemed very worldly indeed and put us both in the proper mood for our entrance into the hotel.

The duc de Morny is credited with having said, "All good Americans, when they die, go to Paris." Had he flourished in the early 1920's, he might have added, "And stay at the France et Choiseul," for sooner or later nearly every itinerant American got there. It was hard to explain its popularity,—it was noisy, the service was not over-efficient, and guests were always being moved from one room to another. But it was conveniently located on the rue St. Honoré. The rooms were attractive and clean, the food good, and the atmosphere pleasant. Mother and I had spent the preceding winter there, so I felt I was an old habituée of the place.

Our veteran chariot with the fierce warrior at the wheel came to a miraculously safe stop. Two France et Choiseul porters—it said so on their caps—ran out to unload our luggage, and the old warrior jumped from his seat to fling open the door for us. This was indeed a different arrival from our humiliating trudge behind the wheelbarrow in Dieppe. So much attention, plus our exhilarating encounter with Emily's school friend, set us up considerably. More-over, we had on our best crêpe marocains and they always gave us a tendency to feel dangerously alluring. With a gracious smile to the driver and a regal nod at the porters, we walked into the hotel as if we had either coronets or books on our heads.

We were met at the *bureau* by Josef, the concièrge. Josef was an amiable soul with a profound interest in the affairs of the entire clientèle. He listened to everybody's telephone conversations, read all the mail he could open, and could tell you to a nicety just where and with whom Mrs. Smith was dining and at what time Mme. Jones had a fitting at Callot's. He was very fond of showing off his English, which was limited, and, to judge by the accent, his teacher must have come from Brooklyn.

Our "Pomp and Circumstance" bearing impressed him, for he gave us a deep, respectful bow, a tribute we almost never received. Then suddenly he recognized me and broke into a roar of delight.

"Ah, c'est la petite Mlle. Skinner!" he informed us and everyone within the radius of a block or two. "Quel plaisir! 'Ow is Momma?" This was humiliating. I worshiped my mother but I didn't want her around on this, the occasion of my first independent arrival at a Paris hotel. And certainly not referred to as "Momma." *Maman* at least would have been "Frenchy." "Momma" made me suddenly feel that I had bands on my teeth.

Josef said he would give us a nice room for the night but next morning he would be forced to move us to another—also nice (we moved four times in two days to rooms which were practically identical) and still talking about "Momma," led the way to that emblem of France, the self-propelling *ascenseur*, into which we all squeezed at once and by some fluke we reached our floor without getting stuck. I remembered this lift well from the winter before. It was about the size of a jury-box and was usually adorned with an out-of-order sign saying *Arrêt momentané*, which meant it wouldn't be working for several days. There was a technique to running it. If you wanted to ride to the fourth floor, you pushed the button for the fifth. The conveyance would make it all right to a foot or two beyond the third, but then would start to falter. To encourage it, you leaned out and eased the load by chinning yourself on the sill of the landing above, at which the capricious apparatus would take a new lease on life and continue on to the fourth. One was warned never to *descendre* in it, because it sometimes got going and ended on the ground floor in a violent bump. But guests sometimes forgot and to soften the impact, straw was packed at the bottom of the shaft. I well remember the night an elderly Philadelphia lady of imposing dignity and size, on her way to the tub, which was on the floor below her room, pushed the wrong button, and clad only in a transparent kimono, descended majestically before the fascinated gaze of the guests in the courtyard.

Our room overlooked the courtyard, a sweet, hidden spot, gay with potted plants. This was the main gathering place, furnished with tables and chairs where one could have drinks,—noisy, but then, too,—cosy. It was later afternoon and people were arriving for cocktails. Emily hung out the window and watched them with awe, the smart men and women of Paris, actual "Parisians," gathering at little tables for a drink before dinner. This was the *beau monde*, all right.

I started to unpack, but she was frantic to get out on the streets. She wanted to find herself suddenly walking down a *boulevard* and she felt like running as fast as she could from the Latin Quarter to Montmartre and out to the Bois de Boulogne to make sure they were really there. I said, very well, we could unpack later. I wanted to see Paris, too, although after all, it was an old story to me. Emily told me such an attitude was just "put on." She was right. I was every bit as feverish to get going as she, and we tidied ourselves up for dinner. We thought it wise not to dress, because if we were out on the streets alone, the two of us in evening clothes, "there might be men."

To reach the dining room, one passed through the court, and Emily was a trifle dashed to discover that the "Parisians" she'd been watching with such reverence were calling to one another about what friends they'd met that day from Connecticut or Keokuk. However, she leapt quickly to a feeling of warm kinship with them—other cosmopolitans like herself.

As I recall, I was quite offensive over that dinner. After all, it was our first in a Paris hotel. (Incidentally, I doubt if this particular hotel had ever seen a French occupant.) I guess I felt it would not be long now before Emily's French improved and I could no longer show off. I demanded to *consulter* with the maître d'hôtel, although Emily said she was doing "just finely" with our own waiter, and what's more, was ravenously hungry. But I had to put on a bit of exhibitionism in rather loud French, accompanied by a lot of shrugs and head tossings which I thought extremely effective until Emily told me to stop acting like a circus pony. We ended up with the regular table d'hôte, roast beef, potatoes and a green vegetable.

After dinner, we would have liked a demi-tasse and cigarette in the court, but decided we'd better go in gradually for such worldliness. Besides, Paris was waiting out there, and it was only a strong sense of decorum which kept us from skipping out through the archway opening onto the rue St. Honoré and "LIFE!" Emily's knees were shaking so, she said, it was doubtful if she could walk, but she made it to the corner of the rue Castiglione. The shops, closed for the night, presented a façade of iron shutters, and with a happy cry of recognition, she exclaimed, "Why, this must be the Bourse!"

"The what?" I asked.

"The Bourse. You know—the Purse, where all the francs are kept."

"These are shops," I said indulgently. "The one you are looking at is the American Drug Store."

She said, "Oh," and went on to the rue de Rivoli. I pointed out the Tuileries with modest pride, as if I'd laid them out myself. Then we reached the Place de la Concorde, and I showed her the beginning of the Champs Élysées. Emily was incredulous. She said she had no idea the Elysian Fields were so near at hand. Not that she was disappointed, but it seemed almost too neighborly. She had always harbored a picture in which, wearing a hat with a willow plume, one drove for hours in a landau, and by and by was joined by a throng of other fashionable people, all pressing in the same direction. Everyone bowed and smiled and then the road widened out. Ahead was a carpet of lush green, and one was at the Champs Élysées.

We weren't wearing willow plumes, and there wasn't a landau handy, but a fiacre was standing outside the Crillon. The *cocher*, an amiable soul with a face like an apoplectic walrus, called out that he was about to turn in for the day, but it was such a lovely evening, he'd drive us to the Étoile and back for half fare. We hopped in with alacrity, the driver unwound his reins, and the tired old horse started clopping doggedly across the Place de la Concorde, past those seated heroines, the cities of France—Metz and Strasbourg, so long in mourning, now festive with wreaths. Swallows wheeled about the obelisk and the rearing horses of Marly looked white and ghostly against the darkening trees. The sloping Avenue rose before us in a soft, blue haze, as if Monet had painted it, and the thick foliage of the *châtaigners* stirred drowsily in the warm evening breeze. It was late twilight, the time of day the French call *la crépuscule*, one of the loveliest words in the world. We didn't talk. Conversation seemed out of place. Ahead of us rose a stolid arch.

"The Arc de Triomphe?" Emily asked, and I nodded.

As we drew nearer, it became more and more majestic, and finally in the dim light we were able to discern the

stark sculpture groups of Rude with the thundering figure
of La France, arms outstretched, mouth wide open as if
crying out, "Aux armes, citoyens!" The driver pulled up
his old beast and asked us if we wouldn't like to get out
for a few minutes. We walked up the steps and stood under
the great span of the largest triumphal arch in the world.
Then we turned around.

"Look," I said and I pointed down the Avenue. "It's the
history of France, that straight line down there. At the
other end is the Louvre, and this is the way to see it for
the first time, standing up here, at the beginning of modern history."

We could just make it out in the soft gloom, the winter
residence of the Kings of France. Halfway between was
the Place of anything but Concorde, where fell so many
of those effete but gallant powdered heads, and where,
later, the little man from Corsica erected the fine bit of
Egyptian booty to the glory of his own name. And here,
at the end of it, in the vast archway, under such names as
Austerlitz, Iéna, Marengo, and Friedland we stood, the two
of us, young and hopeful in the young and hopeful 1920's.
Beside us were the chains let down to make way for a re-
stored Alsace and Lorraine, and in the wavering light of an
eternal flame, we gazed at the grave of an unknown soldier, the common denominator of the course of history.
Now and then shadowy figures moved like ghosts through
the archway. When they passed the resting place of their
unknown comrade, the men took off their hats and the
women silently crossed themselves.

As we stood there, the soft pink street lights flickered
on. Not all of them at once, but starting far off at the
Louvre, then coming on up the Avenue chapter by chap-

ter, from François Ier to the Unknown Soldier, the light
beside him making strange shadows among the battles of
Napoleon.

Slowly we returned down the steps and our eyes were
wet. The old driver was waiting beside his dozing nag. He,

too, had been looking at things and had been having his
own meditations. His shiny leather hat was in his hand.
He observed us shrewdly for a moment and in his husky
voice said,

"Je vous remercie, mesdemoiselles, au nom de la France."

Then with a gesture of ferocity, he clapped his hat on his
head, muttering a stream of complaints about how he and
his horse had been kept waiting there in the night air and
how unreasonable it was to expect a person to stand there
with currents of air rushing about one's head. And he drove
us home.

CHAPTER 10

OUR sojourn at the France et Choiseul was brief. We found it too full of Americans and we had not come abroad, we said, to see Americans. We were poisonously young. We wanted to plunge whole-heartedly into native atmosphere, and, if possible, to talk nothing but French.

The Wallace Irwins were staying at the France et Choiseul and Mrs. Irwin told us about a pension not far from the Étoile where her sister had spent the winter. It was a charming old house, she said, with a garden, good food, and best of all, it was patronized solely by French people. Even her sister had left, so we might count on plenty of atmosphere.

My family had arrived from England and we told them about this picturesque retreat. We had also, however, told Mother about the equally picturesque retreat we had encountered in Rouen and, horrified, she had enlightened us regarding its sinister nature. She and Father became dubious about our powers of discriminating on our own. But we brought up the old Independence Cry, so they journeyed to the Ternes district to see for themselves. It was an attractive place and they approved. "And besides," Mother said, "Letty Irwin is so talented," an obscure recommendation which seemed to clinch the matter.

The morning of our *démenagement*, we received a telegram from our doctor friends, Joe Aub and Paul White,

180

They were arriving in Paris next day; would we go to Versailles that afternoon with them, come back to town for dinner, the theatre, and dancing somewhere afterward? We whooped with joy. This was something *like*, we burbled. Just what it was like, we couldn't have said, but it certainly was *not* like anything that occurred often in our daily lives. Our stabs at intellectual prowess were all very commendable, but let a beau, or even a vague male acquaintance appear, we shed our earnestness as we used to shed our winter underwear at the word of permission. We tried to react to this intoxicating invitation in a blasé manner, but couldn't keep it up, and in no time we were twittering away about our clothes, our hair, and our "line." We went over every detail with the family until Father, unable to bear it any longer, went off alone for an apéritif at the Café de la Paix.

By late afternoon we had effected our move to 6 rue Demours. It was a comfortable and respectable sort of place. Madame Griffe, the proprietress, gave us a pleasant and genteel greeting and allotted us a large room overlooking a charming garden with tall trees shading graveled paths, a few iron tables and chairs, and a crumbling vine-covered wall. The room was agreeably furnished. There was a fireplace with a marble mantel over which hung an ornate Louis XV mirror, for the pension was located in a house which had "seen better days." The most conspicuous piece of furniture was a canopied bed, so enormous it looked as if it belonged at Fontainebleau with a rope around it. We protested to Mme. Griffe that we could not possibly share a bed. She said that was too bad, for it would destroy the symmetry of the room, but if we insisted, she would provide a cot for the night and next day substitute twin beds for that piece of museum grandeur.

My parents took us to dinner but we came back early. Tomorrow was to be a day of days and we must get a good night's rest. Nothing, Emily said, was a greater aid to beauty than a long slumber; the eyes were made clear and sparkling and the skin like tinted porcelain. (She must have gotten that out of Gene Stratton Porter.) With sweet unselfishness she insisted that for the sake of my beauty I sleep in the large canopied affair. I was too long for the cot, and a restless night would be disastrous for my complexion. We water-waved our hair with rigid rows of bristling combs, doing up the side-pieces in painful little steel curlers, and we gave ourselves facials of Daggett and Ramsdell's cold cream. Emily slathered hers on, but I used a patting motion, which I had read somewhere was the method Blanche Sweet used. Then we climbed into our respective beds and switched off the light.

We slept the number of hours requisite for beauty, but sleep didn't do for my eyes and complexion just what I had anticipated. Toward morning, I began feeling restless and curiously uncomfortable. But I managed to doze along till eight, when the sun streamed in the window. Then I woke with a start, knowing that something was definitely wrong. It was my face. It felt as if it were about to split at the cheek-bones. Cautiously I put up a hand to investigate, but my hand stopped several inches away, out beyond my nose. What had stopped it was a great, hot protuberance which seemed to be a blown-out extension of my mouth. I could see it without even looking down. Slowly I sat up in bed and apprehensively raised my eyes to a reflection in the ornate mirror which, I realized with horror, was my own. My upper lip was swollen forth in a fabulous sort of disk—like those of the Ubangi people in the *National Geographic* whose mouths are trained to look like that through years of stretching them over plates. The swelling took up so much of my skin, my eyes were pulled down like a bloodhound's. Everything about my countenance had a high gleam, especially that throbbing upper lip which shone like a polished tomato.

At that moment there was a knock at the door and I dived back under the covers as Jeanne, the *femme de chambre*, came in with *petit déjeuner*. "Bonjour!" she greeted us cheerily. "Ces Mesdemoiselles ont bien dormi?"

"Très bien, merci," Emily chirped back, bright and happy as a bird. I hid under the bedclothes, saying nothing, one bloodhound eye glaring balefully at the maid until she left the room. Then, holding the sheet like a yashmak over the bridge of my nose, I sat up.

"Emily!" I commanded in ringing tones which Duse, Bernhardt and Modjeska never equaled, "LOOK at me!" and I dropped the sheet. It was a staggering unveiling. Emily looked at me as people must have looked at the Gorgon the second before they turned into stone. She started to speak, but the sight of me was something which paralyzed her powers of utterance. At last she was able to croak out in an awed whisper, "What did it?"

"BEDBUGS!" I declaimed and fell back on the pillows.

If I had burst forth in the most lurid blasphemy, Emily could not have been more shocked. The very word, she told me later, was one which a nice person never even uttered. She recalled the time a maid had brought this shame into their Indiana house, a disaster after which "every stick of furniture" in the servant's room had in consequence been burned. But the cause of the holocaust had been mentioned only under bated breath. And here was I, her closest companion, not only saying the word, but attacked by apparent phalanxes of them.

"It's this damned historic bed!" I wailed, and by now I was less Bernhardt than a girl who would bawl any minute.

"And I *always* get bitten and it's *always* on my face! Every species of the insect kingdom bites me, fleas, spiders, flies . . . even moths! And they never bite me anywhere except on the face!"

"Maybe it's the perfume you use," Emily suggested. It was a soothing idea. If I exuded such fascination, I must be pretty fatal. The thought of my powers of seduction, however, reminded me that this was our day for putting them to practice on the young doctors, and at the prospect, I collapsed.

"I'll never see them!" And this time I really did cry, loud and hard. "I'd rather die! And if they ever find out the cause of my disgrace, I'll kill myself!"

This seemed to Emily confused but drastic, and it galvanized her into action. "We're going to the American Drug Store," she said, and leapt out of bed. "They'll tell us what to do. This must have happened before—" although she couldn't believe it had. By way of consolation she added, "And we'll never tell a living soul."

We downed our croissants and café au lait. Even an hour of crisis and disgrace failed to blunt our appetites. Then we dressed with alacrity. Clad, and with my hair fixed, I was even more horrifying to behold. My great blown-out lip gleamed brighter than before, and my eyes took on a Landseer appearance. Whenever Emily looked at me, she went into a curious paroxysm which started in a wild laugh and ended in a sort of hysterical sob. And whenever I caught a glimpse of myself in the mirror, I moaned and looked hastily away. I put on a hat with a wide brim, and again got out the same white veil which had shrouded me through the measles. It seemed to be my idea of protective coloring, so Emily let it go, although it did not cause me to pass unnoticed.

We leapt into a taxi, telling the driver to go as fast as possible. To issue such an order was, we knew, risking our lives, but we were desperate. We had just two hours before the "men" would arrive. The driver, after a shuddering glance at me, covered the distance between the Étoile and the rue de Rivoli in record time and came to a squealing stop. We threw him his fare and shot into the pungent haven of the American Drug Store.

And there, just inside the door, stood Miss Mary Moore Orr of Brooklyn Heights and Gramercy Park. She was an elderly spinster, a friend of Mother's. Very aristocratic and equally rich, she lived at the Crillon, which awed us. She also was the head of the Jardin des Enfants unit in the devastated regions, rehabilitating entire villages, and that filled us with reverent admiration. We were anxious to make a genteel impression on her, for she sometimes took us to tea, or gave us rides in her Rolls Royce. At sight of her, I retired into the recesses of my white veil and Emily stood blocking me from view as best she could.

"Hello, girls," she said cheerily, "what's brought you out so early?" Emily gave her a sickly grin. "I'm just leaving for my villages. My car's outside. Hurry up with your little errands; you can drop me at the station and the chauffeur can take you wherever you like."

Emily began to splutter then, something about not wanting to be a bother, but Miss Orr cut her short, saying she had plenty of time, and ushered us toward the counter.

We urged her not to dream of waiting. We had far too many purchases to make. But she was indulgent and refused to budge. Sparring for time, I bought a washcloth, an orange-stick and a jar of Savon Gibbes—Miss Orr, like Nemesis, hovering close at hand.

Finally Emily hissed, "She'll have to know."

"You tell her," I muttered behind my tomato mouth. "I can't."

"All right," Emily replied. "Only I won't say the word." Leaving me to occupy the clerk, she walked off, beckoning Miss Orr, who followed in amused bewilderment. In the lee of a case of sponges, Emily started whispering.

"Miss Orr," she said, "we are in terrible trouble."

"Why, you poor children." She was still indulgent and kind. "What's the matter?"

"Well,"—Emily wanted to be explicit, without saying the word—"it's really Cornelia. She's the one in trouble physically, but I'm in it, too, of course, because we're together."

"What do you mean?" Miss Orr asked sharply. "Cornelia's in trouble physically?"

"Well, she was—she was attacked last night."

Miss Orr grabbed Emily's arm. "Where?" she asked hoarsely.

"In bed. We just moved in to the pension yesterday and we didn't know about it." She meant the bed.

Miss Orr groaned. "Oh, these French!" She had turned very white.

"We don't want to tell her mother and Mr. Skinner"— Miss Orr nodded her head violently in agreement, but seemed incapable of speech—"but we thought we could get something at the Drug Store—because she's really very badly bitten."

I thought Miss Orr was going to faint, but Emily decided it was better to keep on to the end.

"And isn't there something that will keep them from coming back?"

"*Them?*"

"Yes," she insisted. "Or should we burn the bed?"

I had thought Miss Orr's strength had practically ebbed away, but her eyes snapped open and she leaned over and shook Emily.

"What are you talking about?" she demanded. "*Bedbugs?*"

We shuddered at the word. "Why, yes," I chimed in and

wondered what on earth she *thought* Emily had been talking about.

"Young man!" this scion of old New York roared out to
the clerk. "Make up a gallon of that Lysol solution I take
to my villages and find some of those large brushes. These
young ladies have bedbugs. And give me a chair. I've had a
bad fright." For some reason she appeared to be quite put
out with us both.

She then ordered a lotion for my face and, to my humiliation, made the first application there in the shop. Then, to
my further chagrin, she drove us to the France et Choiseul
and insisted we inform my parents. When she saw me,
Mother cried out in anguish, and Father gasped, "My God,
she's turned into an ant-eater!" They said they'd better
come along and do something right away, and with the
light of battle in their eyes, leapt into the car with us. We
dropped Miss Orr at the station. She was anything but re-
luctant to leave us, and her parting shot was, "Don't ever
do a thing like that to me again!" which we didn't understand at all. Then her car dropped us and our vermin-fight-
ing equipment at the pension.

We set right to work. Father took off his coat, rolled up
his sleeves, announced in ringing tones that he was "Otis,
the Mighty Hunter," and had the time of his life swishing
and swabbing the solution over every bit of woodwork in
the room. Keeping time with his brush, he composed a song
concerning his prowess as a hunter and the elusiveness of
his game. It is a pity we didn't write it down, but we were
occupied ourselves. Mother busied herself poulticing my
face with the lotion which, by a miracle, worked. My lip
deflated, the gleam faded away, and my eyes went back to
normal.

Father having taken over the exterminating situation, Emily and I put our minds on getting ready for the intoxicating day which lay before us, and decided to wear our knitted dresses. These were two gems we'd bought in Dieppe for very little, which was not surprising. In those days, size 14 was big on me, and my model was an ample 40; but I'd taken it for length and because it was marked down. It was white with a sort of waffle pattern across the blouse in a color seldom seen outside of paint boxes. It may have been *rose madder*, or perhaps it was *burnt Siena*, but it was garish. Emily's had also been marked down. The fit was better than mine. It, too, was white, but it must have been originally ordered for someone in mourning, for it was bordered with bands of black, which Emily fancied because she thought they were "old looking."

Jeanne, the *femme de chambre*, came puffing up to inform us that *deux messieurs* were waiting, and we swept down to meet them with beating hearts and an air of nonchalance. After greeting us, Paul and Joe enquired politely about my parents, and we said an early engagement had prevented Mother and Father seeing them. We did not mention the fact that at the moment, they were on their hands and knees upstairs engaged with brushes and a jug of Lysol.

There never was such a day. We went first to Pré Catelan, where, in the shade of a fringed umbrella, we had a lunch beginning with *écrivisses* and ending with *fraises des bois*. An orchestra played thin, seductive tunes ("Mon Homme" was the rage that year) and we felt like pictures out of *Harper's Bazaar*. From there we went on to Versailles, where we made a cursory trip through the show rooms (our avidity for sight-seeing was not so keen when we were "out with men"), we wandered about the parks, and took snapshots of ourselves feeding the carp. Then we drove back to Paris and parted to dress for dinner.

As we ran up the front steps, we could hear the voice of Mme. Griffe engaged in bewildered struggle with another voice, a voice which hailed unmistakably from below the Mason-Dixon line. Emily, hearing it, stopped dead and exclaimed, "That's Mary Miller Brown from Louisville, Kentucky!"

There stood an exquisite little creature with curly blond hair and enormous blue eyes. What she was doing in this exclusively French pension I couldn't imagine, but she had gone to Miss Wright's with Emily, and at sight of one another, they squealed with delight. Then without further ado, the little blonde burst forth with a torrent of words.

"Darlin'," she said, "Ah've got a date for dinner with the cutest man you ever *saw.* Ah can't wait hyeah for John an' Anne. Ah don't rightly know *whut* time their plane gets in. You tell that to Madame *hyeah.* Ah've been yellin' mah lungs out at her, but the louder Ah yell English, the louder she ainswers in French!" and she rushed off. I started upstairs, but Emily felt obliged to convey this obscure message with her fluent vocabulary of "safety valve" and "spitting forbidden." She pointed to the front door through which Mary Miller had blown and said, "Elle est partie," which was apparent and hardly elucidated the situation. But we didn't know who John and Anne were anyway.

We hurried on up to our room. The smell of Lysol came sizzling down two flights of stair to greet us. Otis, the Mighty Hunter, had apparently done a thorough job and the place smelled like several hospitals, but we didn't mind. We had been waiting for this heady moment when we could tell each other everything Paul and Joe had said, and just what we had said back, although not one of us had been more than six feet away from the others the entire day. We were well into it, shrieking about every "killing" witticism and each "terrible faux pas" we'd made, when from across the way came a clamor which topped our own.

Cutting short our shrill confidences, we opened the door and peered into the hall and the face of a young man who stood there clutching the tight curls of his closely-cropped reddish hair. His eyes and accent were the same as Mary Miller's, and we gathered he must be her brother, doubtless that John to whom she'd referred. Mme. Griffe was looking at him in bewilderment as he made abortive attempts to explain something to her in a French which had a high flavor of blue-grass. From a nearby bedroom came a girl's voice, loud and mad, and also from the land of Man-o'-War.

"Listen to me, John Brown," it said. "Ah've grown up with you, an' gone to Sunday school with you, but Ah've never gone to bed with you an' Ah'm not startin' now. You tell that woman to stop showin' us rooms with bigger beds in 'em and get me a room with a bed to myself. Go on now, tell her!"

The owner of the voice stamped out of Mme. Griffe's most seductive double room. It was a girl named Anne Camden, another product of Miss Wright's. Mme. Griffe stood shrugging and making despairing gestures, unable to fathom the behavior of this eccentric couple.

But John Mason Brown, the future eminent critic, author and lecturer, then fresh out of Harvard, met the crisis with the ingenuity and charm with which he now overpowers every woman's club from the Atlantic to the Pacific.

"Madame!" he cried, and the blood of a long line of

Those were the years of the great American Summer migrations, and we were constantly meeting other people "from home." We tried to be strong-minded and avoid our compatriots as much as possible, but our strength of mind varied according to the types of invitations we'd receive. If we were asked to go "dutch" on some sort of all day excursion, we'd decline politely; if it was a question of tea at Columbin's, with the promise of babas-au-rhum and those delectably chewy little madeleines, we'd say, "Well, yes," and if (which was rare) it was a chance for a free meal at a good restaurant, we'd start getting ready then and there.

Social life at the pension was limited. We encountered the other pensionnaires only at meals and most of them ate in silence. They were nearly all *petits commerçants* with a few military and government officials. I remember one retired colonel, very fiercely moustached, a Monsieur Bluet, to whom Emily and I referred with joy in the translation, and quite openly in his presence, as Mr. Cornflower. We were startled when, one day, he turned, and in impeccable Oxford English, asked us to help him verify a quotation. We were again startled the evening Madame ushered into the dining room two new boarders whom she seated next to Emily and me. They were very polite and unobtrusive, but they were also quite black. We gulped a little at this, and Emily said, "Maybe they're Egyptians," which for some reason seemed an optimistic viewpoint. They turned out to be Senegalese dignitaries of sorts, who stayed only two days.

Food at the pension was not particularly bad, nor was it too good, and we decided to enhance it with a bottle of wine. There was a wine shop nearby and not knowing anything about brands or vintages, we one day purchased

ticed fingers, and at other moments, I grew pensive like
Rodin's *Thinker*. What they thought of such curious man-
nerisms, I can't imagine, but there seemed nothing else to

do at the time. To explain what had happened to me would
have been unthinkable. From "Ta Bouche" we went to
Zelli's, where I continued my arch hand-play. We danced
and I swooned about the floor with the lower part of my
face buried in my partner's shoulder. Finally we were taken
home. My mouth felt worse than ever, and at the door of
the pension I shook hands, crooking my elbow about the

lower part of my face in an Egyptian dancer movement which sent the boys off in a mist of speculation.

Next morning, due to more compresses of lotion, my mouth was back to normal. We dressed and started out for a stroll. John Mason Brown was going down the hall ahead of us and we called out to ask how he'd made out with his rooming situation. He hesitated a moment, then turned toward us and only his eyes peeked wildly above his hand. In a muffled tone he informed us his room was all right but he himself had come down with a bad case of hives. To his injured bewilderment we burst into roars of wild laughter, then we explained, and after a stunned moment of revelation, he lowered his hand from his swollen countenance, and he, too, went into howls of delight.

"Comrades," he said, "this is a tie that binds closer than the blood it draws. Friendships have been made today on a kind of bed-rock. Nothing can ever part us."

We shook hands and went together to lunch.

CHAPTER 11

A LTHOUGH John Mason Brown and his sister stayed
at the pension, they never ate a single meal there,
which both shocked and impressed us. We thought
of them as fabulously wealthy. Later we learned that they
had come into some sort of patrimony, and were spending
the entire lump sum on one riotous European holiday, but
at the time we thought of them as nothing short of members of the Vanderbilt or Duke families. Mary Miller
dashed about incessantly with a string of adorers. She
bought dresses at the big houses, and she was constantly
acquiring wonderful hand-made underwear. As for John,
he seemed only a degree less glamorous. He was awfully
Harvard, carried a cane (it was his first and he usually held
it in the middle for fear of tripping over it) and he knew
all about the French theatre. One morning he invited me to
breakfast with him across from the Comédie Française, at
the Café de l'Univers, which was, he assured me, patronized
by all the best actors of the Français. This was indeed a
delirious outing. To be sure, he chose a somewhat curious
time of day. Breakfast is not an ideal hour for actor-watch-
ing, and we went at 9:30 A.M., when even the waiters were
scarcely awake, and the chairs were still piled on top of the
tables. Although we saw nobody remotely resembling an
actor, we gazed with awe at the favorite tables of Cécil
Sorel, Georges Berr, and Berthe Bovy, and felt very bohemian.

Those were the years of the great American Summer migrations, and we were constantly meeting other people "from home." We tried to be strong-minded and avoid our compatriots as much as possible, but our strength of mind varied according to the types of invitations we'd receive. If we were asked to go "dutch" on some sort of all day excursion, we'd decline politely; if it was a question of tea at Columbin's, with the promise of babas-au-rhum and those delectably chewy little madeleines, we'd say, "Well, yes," and if (which was rare) it was a chance for a free meal at a good restaurant, we'd start getting ready then and there.

Social life at the pension was limited. We encountered the other pensionnaires only at meals and most of them ate in silence. They were nearly all *petits commerçants* with a few military and government officials. I remember one retired colonel, very fiercely moustached, a Monsieur Bluet, to whom Emily and I referred with joy in the translation, and quite openly in his presence, as Mr. Cornflower. We were startled when, one day, he turned, and in impeccable Oxford English, asked us to help him verify a quotation. We were again startled the evening Madame ushered into the dining room two new boarders whom she seated next to Emily and me. They were very polite and unobtrusive, but they were also quite black. We gulped a little at this, and Emily said, "Maybe they're Egyptians," which for some reason seemed an optimistic viewpoint. They turned out to be Senegalese dignitaries of sorts, who stayed only two days.

Food at the pension was not particularly bad, nor was it too good, and we decided to enhance it with a bottle of wine. There was a wine shop nearby and not knowing anything about brands or vintages, we one day purchased

something by the eeny-meeny-miny-mo method, toted it
home, and asked to have it placed on our table. It proved to
be very sweet and weak, but that was all the same to us.
To have our own bottle of wine on the table gave, we felt,
an impression that we knew "what was what." After dinner
I had an idea. All Europeans, I said, put a sticker on their
wine bottles to indicate how much had been drunk. Incidentally, the only "European" I had ever seen do it was a
lady from Boston. It was a means of preventing the servants
from tippling. The idea was thrifty and French, and we
felt it would make us appear even more *au courant*. We
went upstairs, cut a piece from the flap of an envelope,
brought it down to the dining room and stuck it on the
bottle. Next evening, I said, we'd put on another label at
whatever new level we'd reached. But the next evening
when we descended with the new sticker, the maître d'hôtel
(who by day was the general handy man) was, as we
opened the door, in the process of lowering with a large
wet thumb, our original sticker to a new level which he
himself had achieved.

Our other alcoholic purchase was a bottle of Benedictine,
because we thought a liqueur after dinner was the proper
thing. We were too embarrassed and too distrustful to have
it also placed on our table, so we kept it in our room, and
after dinner we'd take our toothbrushes out of their tum-
blers, pour out a tablespoonful of Benedictine, pull up
chairs in front of the long window on the garden, light
cigarettes, and swirling the sweet, sticky liquid around—it
barely covered the bottom of the glass—and inhaling gustily
its bouquet—we would talk about THINGS. Ah, *jeunesse
dorée!*

We occasionally passed a pleasant hour or so in the dismal little salon with two young Frenchmen, one of whom was named Jacques Ventadour, the name of the other I doubt if we ever knew. There was an ancient upright piano

in the corner, and to its decrepit jangle, Jacques taught us the tango, while the other lad played a version of the tune, necessarily abridged, as the only music he had was a torn-off half of one sheet. But it sounded all right to us. Young Ventadour was a superb dancer and when we danced with him, we each in turn felt like Florence Walton twirling

about in the arms of Maurice. In return for the tango lessons, we taught the French gentlemen a few American har-
mony gems at which, we prided ourselves, we were "every
bit as good as the Fairbanks Sisters." Our pieces of resist-
ance were "April Showers" and "Avalon," but they preferred our rendition of "You Can't Have Lovin' Where
There Ain't Any Love." We took turns singing alto.

Life, however, was not all frivolity. The Sorbonne was
offering Summer courses *pour les étrangers*, and we en-
rolled, Emily because she thought it would improve her
French quicker than the memorizing of printed signs, and
I because I was agog for culture. We attended the same lec-
tures from nine to twelve. Then I took an extra one, partly
for good measure, and partly because I was rather taken
with a Norwegian youth who attended that session. He
used to hold my coat and open doors for me, and during the
lecture hour, would gaze at me with an intensity which
made me quite nervous, but pleased me beyond measure.
As he spoke no English and never learned any French, and
as I was certainly not up in Norwegian, the romance never
got very far. However, it was reason enough for my staying on for that extra hour. Emily generally waited for me
across the street at the Cluny Museum. And it was thanks
to the Cluny Museum that Emily learned about Life.

It is hard to believe how little we knew about that all-
absorbing subject. In comparison with the modern generation, ours was an innocence which bordered on arrested
development. Emily's and my children at the ages of eleven
and twelve know and have known for five or six years as
much as we knew at that guileless period. I pretended to be
more versed in these matters than Emily, but that was sheer
affectation. Other and more precocious girls our ages may

have "found out about things," but we were not precocious. As I look back on it, we weren't even very bright.
It was not, either, that our mothers were Victorian prudes.
They were both of them wise and brilliant women. The
most vivid and wittiest I shall ever know, Emily always says
of hers; my mother was less incisive, but with an overwhelming store of knowledge. Both of them slaved over
our educations, and had an identical standard of values
about what was important and what was not. And they had
never included in their curricula for us the story of the
birds, bees and flowers. I had a few vague notions, all quite
incorrect. As for Emily, if she thought about such things at
all, her impression of the function of a male parent was that
it built, and brought food to, the nest.

But the Cluny was to open new vistas for her. Wandering there one day in an aimless fashion, gazing at the same
exhibits for the third or fourth time, something caught her
eye. It was that exquisite but frankly realistic carving of
Leda and the Swan. She had looked at it often, but now she
looked at it again. For a moment the world stood still, then
knowledge began to dawn, and she was like a pinwheel that
has just been touched off. Stars, sparks and flames were
bursting in her consciousness, and with wide eyes which
saw nothing, she staggered on to the next room. When her
eyes focused it was upon one of those well-known medieval
objects adopted by the Crusaders as a measure for preserv-
ing the sanctity of the home. And at that, the stars and
sparks became more intense, and she felt she was wheeling
round and round.

"So that's how it is!" she exclaimed aloud, to the surprise
of the guard, and ran back to Leda and the Swan. After
gazing there a few minutes she said, again aloud, "Wait a

minute," to Leda, and rushed back to the other objet d'art.

When I arrived she was running like a bird dog between the two cases, and another sightseer, an Englishwoman, was saying to her companion:

"How disgustingly American! Only interested in the sensational."

Emily muttered, "You *bet* I am!" and seeing me, hailed me with an excited, "Come and see what I've found."

I, to show my superiority, merely said, "Why, of course."

But I pored over the cases pretty breathily myself, and did quite a little bird dog running on my own account.

Emily's second lesson in fundamentals was not quite as graphically illustrated. She had been out to tea with some friends who lived on the Left Bank, an American couple who felt the urge to spend a year in a Paris *atelier*. To be sure, neither of them painted, sculpted or even played a musical instrument. But they made up for any lack of their own creative abilities by keeping open house for most of the artistic riff-raff then so prevalent in the city. Among their enthusiasms was an earnest group from a pseudo-Russian ballet which was performing at one of the smaller "art" theatres—short-haired girls named Masha or Tania, and long-haired lads named Igor or Dmitri, most of them hailing from Chicago. The day she went there for tea, Emily met two of the young men. She found them interesting, but slightly unusual, and when she later joined me and the family at the latter's rooms in the France et Choiseul, she couldn't wait to tell us all about them.

"They were so different from the men I know," she said, "although they were very pleasant. They laughed a lot and they seemed to be wonderfully good friends. I sat between them and they kept leaning across, and talking so eagerly to each other."

Father, who had been reading the theatrical newspaper

Commoedia, at this point looked up over his glasses. Emily, encouraged by his interest, continued, "Wasn't it odd? They both had rouge on and eye shadow." Father made an odd choking sound. "But then I learned that they were from the theatre. I imagine they must have just come from a matinée and hadn't bothered to take off their make-up.

You know," and Emily turned on Father her most social smile, "you've probably done the same thing lots of times yourself."

Father rose, and his wrath was equaled only by that of Achilles. "Never say a thing like that again as long as you live, Emily Kimbrough!" he thundered at her.

She gazed at him blankly. If he had suddenly gibbered and started making faces she couldn't have been more dumbfounded.

"My make-up belongs to my profession and my profession is *inside* the theatre. Maud!" And he roared at Mother, who was sitting there making her little cooing noises of distress. "TELL her!"

He flopped back into his chair like Salvini after the last act of Othello, and picking up the *Commoedia*, read it savagely upside down.

Mother took a deep, sad breath. Then she said, "Come, girls," and led us into the next room. She sat Emily down beside her on the bed, and gently patted her hand.

"Darling," she said, with a catch in her voice. Mother always got emotional in matters pertaining to "life." "Mr. Skinner was upset because what you said showed a certain lack of understanding, and so I want to explain a few things to you."

Here she paused in search of the proper words, while Emily and I, not knowing what else to do, sat there looking the way we did when we'd been sent for by the principal. There was a pause and Mother went on, "Darling, you know who Oscar Wilde was?"

Emily nodded, too bewildered to speak.

"You know, I suppose, that he was sent to prison, poor man, poor tragic man."

Mother hung her head at the thought, but Emily brightened.

"Certainly I know," she said. She began to feel once again on home ground. After all, this was literature.

"Well," said Mother, and her voice was hushed and fearful, "do you know what he was in prison for?"

"Of course," said Emily with loud eagerness. "Debt."

Mother patted her hand again a long time. Finally she spoke very soothingly.

"Well, not exactly, dear. At least not entirely. You see, there are unfortunate people in this world who do not conform in their behavior to that of others. It isn't their fault, but still society can't condone it. So you see, it makes it very difficult and unpleasant. And that is why you must not say such things. And now that I've explained it all to you, I'm sure you never will again."

And we went out of the room, feeling that even if we had not quite grasped the essentials, this had all been extremely momentous.

We found other things, however, a much more disturbing element than sex. Clothes, for one thing. Our budgets allowed for a limited outlay, but we were determined not to "buy a stitch" until just before we sailed for home. Moreover, we were doing a little "couturing" ourselves, and very pleased with it.

I was fairly handy with a needle, and dresses, according to my variety of "couture," were not difficult. That was the era of high, straight-across necks, "kimono" sleeves, and a waist line formed by a belt clasped somewhere around the lower hip. I could run up a dress in an afternoon, exactly the way one might run up a big bag, and I urged Emily to try. All one need do, I told her, was sew up the sides, leav-

ing holes for the sleeves, cut another for the neck, bind the
openings, hem the bottom, and finish it off with a good-
looking ready-made belt. Although the majority of my cre-
ations followed this simple pattern, I had succeeded in ac-
complishing one chef d'oeuvre, which was my pride and
joy. This was an evening dress of fireman's red crêpe, made
particularly "stunning" by bunches of gold grapes at shoulder and hip. To get into it, I had to spread it out along the
floor and after straddling it, lean over and pick up the front.
Then, legs apart, I swayed backwards like a circus tumbler,
and scooped up the back. The pieces snapped together at
the top, and a few extra "drapes" concealed the fact that
my legs were on the outside of the dress.

Emily said that such a pattern was a little involved for
a beginning, but she thought she could manage one of the
bags with holes for neck and arms. She bought three yards
of golden brown velours at the Bon Marché and although
she vowed it was intended for dress material, it looked
rather more intended as upholstery fabric for a davenport.
It was hard to cut, and harder to sew with anything more
delicate than a sail-maker's needle. But nothing daunted,
she set to work. I suggested she spread the stuff on the floor,
lay one of her dresses on top of it for a pattern, and cut it
out accordingly. I said nothing about making allowances
for seams, and as it has always been difficult for Emily to
make allowances for anything unless expressly told to do
so, she cut the goods the exact measurement of the other
garment. As a result, the dress was "skin tight," the sort of
skin a snake sheds in Spring, only instead of sliding *out*, she
had to wriggle into hers. For trimming, she purchased a
chain belt, set with extremely imitation turquoises. The belt
was as loose as the dress was tight, and as Emily's hips were

negligible, it had an unfortunate way of slipping off and rattling down about her ankles, forming unexpected fetters over which, if she wasn't careful, she tripped.

She was proud of her handiwork, however, and the moment she had drilled the last stitch, she put on the creation, a good deal like an umbrella case, and announced that we would go to tea at Columbin's to celebrate. She was dubious about her ability to eat any cakes, but we could at least bring some home, and she was only going to show off her dress, anyway. We did go to Columbin's to tea, but instead of the characteristic little packages of petits fours looped on our forefingers, we came home with two dogs.

They were toy Belgian Griffons, and we spied them in the window of a pet shop, a few doors from Columbin's. In London we had seen for the first time a miniature Belgian Griffon. The tiny canine won our hearts and we began longing for one. In Paris we had haunted every pet shop, but found no Griffons. Wire-haireds were the "rage" that Summer and every Frenchwoman had one named "Mike," "Tommee," or "Beel." But wire-haireds were common in America, while to return with a Griffon would be both chic and spectacular—like Irene Castle and her monkey.

The moment we saw the enchanting little beasts, we knew we'd have to buy them even if the expense meant working our way home on a cattle boat. Emily's was named "Gamin" and mine was "Lili." The woman who ran the pet shop said of Lili, "Vous voyez comme elle est gaie, vive, et de bonne caractere."

At the moment, tiny Lili was backed into a corner, goggle-eyed and shivering with fright.

Lili soon got over her fright, however, and was adorable. I never regretted buying her. As for Gamin, he was Emily's heart's delight for seven years. But at the beginning, we had our troubles, breaking first the news to Mother, then the dogs to the leashes. Mother was outraged at such extravagance. To be sure, Emily had purchased Gamin by means of a special book of American Express checks her grandfather had given her in order to "buy something she wouldn't otherwise get." But Mother thought she should have spent the money on an artistic Babani coat, which, she said, was of such beautiful material it could always be used for something else, and Gamin, obviously, had not that advantage. But she was slightly mollified when she beheld his little cosmos face, and capitulated completely when she saw Lili, who went straight to her heart, and she soon got accustomed to the idea.

To accustom the dogs to their leashes was far less simple. We had bought ravishing little collars with bells on them, and tiny matching leads which charmed us, but not their wearers. The minute they were fastened on, the little hellions, bracing their wee paws, yanked and pulled until their heads came completely out of their collars. Sometimes they did it violently, sometimes so subtly we found ourselves walking happily along, dragging empty collars, in the innocent belief that the creatures were trotting obediently behind us. But that was a vain hope, for they never trotted. They sat on their stubborn rears, and in order to budge them at all, we walked backwards down the Champs Élysées, bent over double, holding tidbits before them, like hay before recalcitrant donkeys. Whenever, unable to bear the strain, we'd straighten up, and, tugging the leashes, walk forward a few steps, some indignant Frenchwoman would threaten to report us to the Société Humaine. We'd turn around and gaze into the upturned faces of Gamin and Lili, grinning malevolently, and behind them for yards, a swathe of gravel scraped by their rears. And then one day, as if they realized we had reached the limit of endurance, those two Belgian torturers rose up on their four legs, and from that moment on, trotted smartly along as if they had been trained to the show ring all their lives.

After that, we took them with us everywhere and always displayed them when we went to restaurants. Aside from making us feel as mondaine as all get out, they were the means of our getting wonderful service. At sight of them, head waiters rushed us to the best table and hovered over our pets, bringing up saucers of minced goodies, and giving us pointers on the feeding of *les p'tits chiens délicats*. (They were about as *délicat* as Eskimo huskies.) But we created a great deal of notice, which was lovely.

One day we decided we owed it to our dogs and ourselves to have lunch at the Ritz. This was a daring move. We were fairly conscientious about eating most of our meals at the pension, and if ever we did indulge in a mild spree, it was to some one of the branch Duval's, or, to be truly giddy, the Franco-Italian on the Rond Point. The Ritz was well beyond our budget but we exonerated ourselves by saying that a luncheon there was part of a European education. So, one day, we took a deep breath and went right in.

We were clad in our best home-mades. Mine was a "slinky" black satin (again the Theda Bara motif) and Emily wore her davenport velours. As we stood in the doorway of the dining room, we were moderately assured of our superior appearance. But lest such superiority might not be instantly recognized, we held up the dogs in front of us. (Emily held up her belt too so that it wouldn't fall down.)

We were immediately greeted by the major domo—in the case of the Paris Ritz it must be the *Field Marshal Domo*. He had noticed us at once. I think anyone was apt to notice us. Making little crooning noises over Gamin and Lili, he led us to one of the best tables and seated us, all four, on chairs of pale rose brocade. We thanked him, and assured him that the little dogs were accustomed to being on the floor, but he said he wouldn't hear of it. He loved Griffons profoundly. He had owned one for fourteen years, and of all animals, they were the most beautiful and the best behaved in the world. He served us lunch himself, brought up dishes of chopped filet mignon for our mascots, and we ate under the rapt scrutiny of every other occupant of the dining room. There may have been celebrities and members of royalty also lunching there, but the guests had eyes for nobody but us. The food was delicious, but we couldn't make the most of it. I was too embarrassed to eat much, and Emily was not only embarrassed, she was afraid that any undue pressure might make the seams of her dress give way.

An imposing dowager at a nearby table had been focusing her lorgnette on Lili with such enchanted admiration and cries of *que tu es adorable, que tu es ravissant, mon petit chou,* that toward the end of the meal, I couldn't resist picking her up, with the pride of a fatuous mother, the better to show her off. I hadn't lifted her five inches before I hastily dropped her back again, for there in the center of the pale rose brocade, was a small, round puddle. Emily, who caught a fleeting glimpse of it, was even more mortified than I. Then as the dowager's lorgnettes veered in her direction, she, too, became the fatuous mother, and held up Gamin to be admired. Five inches above the chair, she hastily put *him* down again, for under him was the twin of

Lili's puddle. We sat there, silent and horrified, not knowing what to do. We lingered endlessly over our coffee, hoping that maybe, as Emily optimistically suggested, it might just dry up. But that brocade must have been *imperméable*. Finally we called for the bill, paid it and rose. Emily seized her little *chou* with one hand and with the other dropped a napkin over the tell-tale seat, and I on my side of the table went through the same motions, as if it were a sister act we had done for years. We managed to make a fairly dignified exit as far as the hall, but from there we scooted like rabbits across the lobby and out the main door. For years to come, I never passed the front door of the Ritz without experiencing the uncomfortable feeling that an irate *Field Marshal Domo* might spring forth, seize me, and make me pay for two brocade chairs.

Next time we ventured into that elegant hostelry, it was via the rue Cambon and into the bar. Nor did we go entirely on our own. Mother, who by now had left Paris on a trip with Father, had bequeathed us, as a chaperone, a strange old spook named Madame Venuat. I can't imagine how Mother acquired her in the first place, unless possibly through the Ladies' Rest Tour booklet. But my parent found her instructive. She had at one time been secretary to the Academician Emile Faguet, a distinction which made her seem rather wonderful to Mother, who was always impressed by that superior element she termed vaguely as "learning." They used to read plays and "do conversation" together, and Mother insisted that we take her on because she was "so good for our idioms." To sit closeted in our room while Mme. Venuat went over the finer aspects of the subjonctif-plus-que-parfait was too much like tutoring for College Boards, so Emily and I used to combine her with sight-seeing. We would take her along to churches and museums, where she would deliver rhetorical little homilies to which we listened or didn't, according to our mood. We usually finished up these excursions at some tea-room, for the way the poor soul lit into the cakes and sandwiches made us realize it was her one meal of the day. At his death, Faguet had left her a tiny bequest by means of which, plus the lessons she gave for very little, she was able to maintain herself and her cat in a dingy garret somewhere off the boulevard Montparnasse.

She was hardly a type for the Ritz bar. Her clothes, which were frayed and spotty, looked as if she'd bought them at a rummage sale. Her hair, dyed the shade of stove polish, was always falling in wisps. She covered her wrinkled face with a dead white powder, and the heavy make-up about her eyes must have been applied with a burnt cork. But we took her there that day because we were dying to go, and were too scared to venture in alone.

Dear knows why we thought that one of the chief high spots in a girl's life was to go to the Ritz bar. Certainly it was the smokiest hole of Calcutta ever conjured up out of an old coat closet. But we stepped across its threshold experiencing a pleasant series of those nervous thrills the French call *frissoms*. We would have had a few more if, instead of Madame Venuat, we had found ourselves accompanied by a French marquis and a polo player from the Argentine, but we murmured to ourselves that "those days will come," and sat down uncertainly at a dim corner table. The bar, I think, was across the hall. There wasn't one in the room. We leaned back against the wall and ate overflowing handfuls of peanuts while we tried to think of what to order. Mme. Venuat wasn't much help. She had obviously never tasted *le cocktail* and she read off the list of mixed drinks in her hoarse, penetrating voice, commenting learnedly upon the derivation of each name. Everyone in the small room stared at us and we were fairly harassed until Providence stepped in in the person of Mary Miller Brown. She was exhausted after a three hours' fitting at Doucet's and needed reviving. She flopped down at our table and we cried gaily, "What'll you have?" which sounded, we felt, sophisticated. It also sounded alarmingly liberal and we had not counted on such additional expense, but Mary Miller was kudos worth paying for.

"An Alexander," she said, and we all, even Mme. Venuat, said that that was just what we were about to order. To be sure, none of us had the faintest notion, outside of a conqueror, what an Alexander was.

The things arrived and it was either a comment on the lack of development of our palates or a proof of our abstemious habits that we tasted that rich, sweet concoction of brandy, crème de cacao and straight cream and found it delicious. We sipped with delight and kept on shoveling in handfuls of peanuts.

In the midst of this epicurean debauch, John Mason Brown arrived, rather suddenly. I don't believe he was much in the habit of patronizing the Ritz bar alone, for he seemed inordinately relieved and pleased to see someone he knew. After his first inrush, he strolled over to us, very casual and handsome and Harvard.

"What are you all having?" he asked and we said "Alexanders" as nonchalantly as we could, only in chorus. He beckoned a waiter with his cane, an impressive gesture. I realize now, it must have been because he had forgotten to check it.

"Alexanders all around," he said. "Et un de plus pour moi."

We hastened to say NO, that we didn't want another. I wasn't sure that I wanted the one I had. But John was firm and lordly. He wanted to "treat" and he was going to "treat." Moreover, the waiter had gone off to fill the order. We became indignant and not a little alarmed, for we'd "begun to feel" the first Alexander, and to risk a second after several pecks of peanuts, was playing with fire. We were firm and said no *sir*, we weren't going to have any more. And our stubbornness made him mad.

"Very well," he said with hauteur, "if you all won't accept my hospitality, I shall treat myself and drink them all!"

That scared the living daylights out of us and we begged him not to do anything so crazy. But he wouldn't listen. The cocktails arrived and, with injured dignity, he picked up the first and downed it. Then, without pausing, he drained off a second. With awful fascination, and in pin-dropping silence, we watched him top off five of the sickening mixtures, one right after another. Then we waited. But not for long. He had hardly finished the last drop before he stood up. His face was a malarial green, his eyes bulged and his cheeks blew out like an allegorical drawing of Aeolus. From afar, he groped for the check, but to lower his head and focus his eyes on it, seemed too difficult, so he handed it over to Mary Miller, together with his cane. He forced himself to give us a dreadful grin, and a dying swan wave of the hand. Then he pulled himself to attention and, in a wan imitation of a West Point cadet on parade, marched from the room and disappeared around the corner.

We sat for a few minutes in stunned speculation. Mme.

Venuat said poor young man, it was the fault of American Prohibition. Mary Miller wanted to be furious at him, but she was too frightened. When we could speak, we thought we'd better go see what had happened to him, so we pulled ourselves together and divided up the bill. By this time Emily and I were past caring what we were spending. We tried to saunter out of the room, but our gait was more of a scuttle. At the threshold, we paused and peered apprehensively around the corner. We thought we might find his body there. But the hallway was empty and it was not until we were out on the street that we saw John again. He was lying back in a taxi which was parked just outside the rue Cambon entrance. The greenish tinge of his face had faded to alabaster white, and his eyes were closed. As we watched, they opened, and with difficulty fixed themselves on the taxi meter. He tried to say something to the driver, but the effort was apparently too great, so he shook a fist at him, after which he collapsed again. We thought this behavior the most alarming we'd seen yet, especially since the driver had turned around in his seat and was looking on with the most sympathetic watchfulness. In a moment, however, things became more clear. For at the first droop of John's eyes, the sympathetic driver seized the flag of the meter and spun it round and round with a rapturous smile. Every turn rang a little bell, and every ting of the bell marked an *up* in the fare. It was this sound which would rouse John, near death as he was, to such righteous protest as he could muster.

We were afraid to interfere, and anyway, Mary Miller said she'd take charge of things. So we left them there in front of the Ritz, the cab still quite stationary. But by the reckoning on the meter, John was far, far beyond the outskirts of Paris.

CHAPTER 12

THE preceding winter I had studied with Dehelly of the Comédie Française. He was one of its leading *sociétaires*, which meant he owned a share in the profits of the National Theatre itself, but he augmented his income considerably by giving diction lessons to a large portion of all the American girls who came to Paris, instructing them in the proper use of vowel sounds, and training their Anglo-Saxon palates in the intricacies of the letter *r*. To me, possibly because my aim was the theatre, he gave more specialized attention. He put me through a rigorous course of classical sprouts, making me memorize everything from La Fontaine's simplest fable to Phaedre's most fulminating speech. His method was excellent, his diction perfect, and I thank my stars I had the opportunity of studying with this man who, if not one of the greatest actors of all time, was certainly one of the greatest teachers. The family had presented me with a check large enough to cover some additional lessons that summer. But I was romantic, and while I adored M. Dehelly, my secret passion (secret, that is, only as far as he was concerned, for certainly I told it to everybody I met) was a player named Jean Hervé, also of the Comédie, whose specialty was parts like *Hernani*, the *Cid*, and those hairy Roman heroes of Racine and Corneille. He was a very actory actor with curly, passionate locks, a flashing eye and a ranting delivery, but I thought he was just lovely, and lavished upon

legs slipped under and the back smacked forward smartingly against her rear. She was catapulted off into space
and as soon as she reached the ground went hurtling
through the crowd, down hill, like an avalanche, while the
chair, like Jill, came tumbling after. She is under the impression that several people were slightly hurt, but no one
was more shaken than she. Some men carried her back up
the hill, set her on her feet, dusted her off and retrieved her
hat which had rolled in another direction. She could walk,
although it was painful, and she decided she would go back
to Paris without waiting for any more races. The ticket,
however, was still in her hand, and when she discovered it,
she hobbled over to the window, though she doubted if
anything would come of it—there must be a fluke somewhere. Two hundred and eighty francs came of it, and she
almost fainted from shock and weakness.

No one else was going back to Paris at that hour. The
station was deserted except for an agent who seemed
amazed that anyone should want to leave before the finish
of the races, and vague in regard to time-tables. He murmured something about a train in five minutes, but he
doubted if she'd want to take it. She asked why not, didn't
it stop, and he said yes, it did stop, but he did not know
if Mademoiselle would find it suitable. And he fluttered his
hands. Emily, who thought that this was the silliest thing
she had ever heard a station agent say, went out on the platform to wait for the unsuitable train.

In just a minute or two it arrived, looking like any other
train, and she limped hurriedly along, in order to be near a
compartment door at the moment of *arrêt*, which by now
she had learned was merely a sudden clashing of cars with-

M. Hervé, I gathered he hadn't been to bed much before seven. He didn't look at all the way he did as the *Cid*, in all that velvet and armor, and I was just as glad he wasn't wearing any of his more dégagé Roman togas. He plumped me onto a straight chair against the wall, gave me a poem of Alfred de Vigny to read aloud, and all the time I was doing so, he himself talked on the phone loud and long, making arrangements about his forthcoming tour. I finished the poem, and he said it was very good and to go on and read another. I am sure he never heard a syllable, of what I said. However, I stumbled on, feeling awfully let down, somehow. A nervous little light, one of those glaring French bulbs, set squarely in the center of the ceiling without any sort of shade, kept flashing on and off. I couldn't make out what was causing it to do so and was a good deal distressed when I discovered it was my own hair net (Venida double-mesh) which had caught around the button on the wall, and at the least movement of my head, snapped it on or off.

After charging me a fair price for this session, Monsieur Hervé departed for his Belgian tour and I didn't see him again for several weeks. Somewhat cured of my *grande passion*, I then returned to my former maître, Dehelly. Emily, who believes in trying out everything, whether it's a new school of thought or a different brand of ice cream soda, said she wished she might take a few diction lessons too. I said I wasn't sure but maybe due to some seductive persuasion on my part, and a possible wild whimsey on that of M. Dehelly, he might condescend to take her on as a pupil. I never told her about the several score of other Americans he had condescended to take on also. But I said I'd drop him a note. The prospect set Emily's teeth clacking in a nervous chill of excitement.

They clacked even more when a reply came from the great man, saying he was happy to give me some more lessons and would consider Emily, and in the meantime, offered his loge for the next afternoon's performance. In a postscript he told me to bring my friend backstage after the last curtain.

To attend the most famous theatre in the world as guests of one of its leading actors and later to be allowed backstage—these were Alpine heights for us both. I was born and brought up in the theatre, but I trust the day never dawns when it ceases to be for me a realm of enchantment. My heart pounds when I go back to see even my close friends, and the very smell of the dust is sweeter than all the perfumes of Arabia, Coty or Houbigant. And it is so with Emily. She saw her first play at the age of seven, at the Wysor Grand Opera House in Muncie, and she says her breath still comes fast and her hands turn cold that moment when the house goes dark and the footlights glow on a curtain about to rise. The curtain in Muncie had advertisements on it of the Owl Drug Store and Sterling's Cash Grocery, but back of it was another curtain with a dazzling picture of ladies in party dresses, zooming about in a swing made of roses. And behind that were Montgomery and Stone in the Wizard of Oz, and she learned what magic was.

It was a long way from the Wysor Grand to the Comédie Française. No wonder she was dizzy. We both were. I hustled her through lunch and true to form, we arrived long before the doors were open. The matinée was advertised to start at "14 hours" and we arrived about "13 o'clock." I was all for standing about under the portico, so as to be among the first inside, but Emily suggested, somewhat caustically, I thought, that if we waited at the café across the street, we could watch the crowds, and

since the show wouldn't start for an hour, we could, barring accidents, get back those few hundred feet in time.

I complied somewhat reluctantly, and for a time we sat at the café sipping that innocuous, sickly drink, a Vermouth cassis, and watching a traditional French audience arrive for a traditional *Matinée Classique.* We have no equivalent for such a gathering, unless this was the Gallic version of the sort of audience which habitually turned out to see Marlowe and Sothern. Respectable members of the *bonne bourgeosie*, they were all in black, men, women and most of the children. The frocks of the little girls were very short, so were their sleeves and they wore short white gloves and prim elastics on their plain turned-up hats. They might have modeled for Boutet de Monvel, for all the change in their type of clothes since the first decade of the century. They were such *French* French children, one felt surprised not to see them each carrying a hoop.

The doors opened and we joined in the rush for seats. Monsieur Dehelly, in presenting his loge, had sent us merely a *laissez passer* slip of paper which we were supposed to turn in at the box office in exchange for those fluttering strips of trans-continental railroad fares, French subscription tickets.

There was no systematic line-up at the Français any more than there ever was for a bus, the Metro or a bargain sale at the Trois Quarters. People merely crowded about the entrance in bee-swarm formation and eventually, due to pressure from either side, some individual in the center would be shot forth and the professors behind the "bureau of location" would give him their academic attention.

Frenchmen in public crowds do not intentionally knock women down. Veneration of woman is a national trait, that is, provided woman stays in her proper environment—the *foyer*, the salon, the restaurant, always, of course, with a male escort and preferably engaged in that agreeable pastime known as *le flirting*. But a woman alone, or with another woman (which is the same thing) should never be catching a bus or buying a ticket. To see her amid such surroundings is unromantic. A Frenchman feels it is more romantic to act as if she were not there. So he pushes her down, if he can.

Somehow, we insinuated ourselves into the wedge and finally, like marbles in an over-jammed box, popped out in front of the box-office window, which wasn't a window at all, but a high desk like a night counter in a station back home, only it was elevated and behind it, instead of Pullman conductors, sat three solemn gentlemen in silk hats. We shoved the *laissez passer* over the counter, thinking to be given our tickets immediately. But that was a fantastic hope. It had first to be passed on by the three oracles sitting there so solemn and portentous, we had an idea they must be the persons who also passed on applications for the Légion d'Honneur. The first man read aloud every word of Monsieur Dehelly's slip of paper to the middle man, who approved it and read it aloud to the third dignitary who wrote it all down in a big ledger with a corroded pen, once pointed, now split like an olive-fork. This, of course, took quite a little time, but we had plenty to spare.

Finally we were allowed to pass on inside, and being among the firstcomers, were easy prey to the Draculas lying in wait. These are the old women, technically known as *ouvreuses*, and it is our firm belief they live all their lives in the theatre, hanging by their toes from the ceiling until an hour or so before a play begins. Then they swoop down with blood-curdling hisses, to sell programmes and exact their own special *bénéfices*, which is a remuneration they expect you to give them for being permitted to sit in the seat you have bought and paid for, whether they have shown you there or not. On their withered heads they wear horrid baby bonnets trimmed with pink bows, despite the fact that these harpies are hundreds of years old and blind from hanging up among the rafters. They cannot make change, but they stand over you, squealing and chattering until you have succeeded in driving them away by giving them a lot of money for their nuisance value. If their victims are late, they can, of course, extort much more because they make such a shrill noise half the audience rises and spits, "Sh-h-h!" so violently the actors can't possibly make themselves heard above the din, and the wretched late-comer will give all he has, including his watch, to be allowed to slink forgotten into his seat.

Monsieur Dehelly's loge was in the center of the house, which meant it was very smart. It also meant that like the best boxes at the New York Metropolitan, it was a long way from the stage. Sitting there, just the two of us, in a box intended for six, we felt very exposed, especially when two men, three rows ahead of us, stood up, turned around and stared at us through their opera glasses. Emily wanted to pull up the latticed *jalousie*, but I wouldn't let her, because, I explained, you only sat behind that if you were a married woman and had come there with your lover.

The play was a Molière comedy, and Monsieur Dehelly, who wouldn't see fifty again, was playing his habitual role of the young lover . . . Dorante or Clitandre, one of those curly boys who wave lace handkerchiefs and bow very low, skip and cavort and sigh, and, in the end, get the girl. I had seen the play before, which gave me an annoyingly superior attitude, rather as if I'd written it. Emily was less blasé. She did not understand a word of it (at that fashionable distance it was next to impossible to hear) but she loved every moment and kept whispering, "To think we're going to meet him! Do you suppose I'll really be able to make an impression on him?"

The curtain came down amid the usual storm of applause tempered by the mechanical beat of the hired *claque*.

"Come along," I said. "We're going backstage."

I led the way. I had been there before and with elaborate assurance I pushed open a door behind the right hand boxes. Tremulous, Emily followed. The only "backstage" she knew were the glimpses she had had on the occasions when Father played in Buffalo or Philadelphia and we both had gone behind to see him. That was a very different "backstage," and she was unprepared for the palatial splendor of the Français, the paneled walls, the thick Aubusson carpets, the portraits by Largillière, Nattier and Ingres. For a moment she stared, then said, "We're in the wrong place." She explained later, she thought we had stumbled upon a set for the evening show. Then, a glass case containing a few exhibits in the way of prompt-books, autographs, and the dainty slipper of Rachel, made her realize she was in the green-room of the National Theatre of France. At the Français, after all, there was no question of a run of several weeks, then on to the next town. Once admitted, an actor played here until retirement. And this lovely, dignified room was the main salon of his professional home where he received his friends and admirers.

Monsieur Dehelly came up, all blond wig, lace ruffs, patches, and other Louis XIV accessories, looking as if he might have stepped out of one of the cases. Not having met for several months, he and I greeted one another with many rapturous flourishes and *Comment ça VA's!!* Then I remembered Emily and her desire not only to meet the distinguished actor, but to make an impression on him. I turned, and with a sweeping gesture, said, "Monsieur, puis-je vous présenter mon amie, Mademoiselle Kimbrough?"

Monsieur bowed with courtly charm and his yellow curls brushed across her hand as he kissed it.

"Mademoiselle," he said, in a low rich voice. And Emily in a throaty vibrant voice solemnly echoed back, "Mademoiselle!"

Emily explained to me later that this was the ultimate peak,—the beautiful room, the Molière manuscript, the famous portrait of Rachel, and then this actor himself all done up in the very period, brushing his golden curls over her hand. At the moment, however, she did not explain anything to me, or to M. Dehelly. And she never spoke again. There was no need, after all. She had made her impression.

Monsieur took us up in the tiny *ascenseur* to the Étage Talma, (instead of being numbered, each floor bears the name of a great actor . . . Étage Bernhardt, Étage Mars, etc.) and bowed us into his dressing room, which was really a suite. We sat in a charming little library in front of an open fire. Monsieur and I chatted busily, but Emily just sat there smiling vacuously at first one then the other.

After a time we left. Dehelly did not kiss Emily's hand again. He seemed to contemplate it, then thought better and merely bowed, a motion which Emily again echoed back.

But he did take her on as a pupil. She thought it extraordinary of him to have recognized her talent hidden beneath the handicap of their first meeting, and went drifting about in a mood of dreamy elation. (She didn't hear about the other American pupils until much, much later.) He sent us appointments for our first lessons along with assignments of things to memorize. Emily was given the first five stanzas of de Musset's "Nuit de Mai," while I was told to come equipped with La Fontaine's "Oak and the Reed." This was a keen disappointment to me. I would have preferred the renunciation scene from "Za-za." But I consoled myself with the thought that Monsieur had once told me only the finest artists could interpret La Fontaine. It must be fluid, he said, yet resonant, every syllable a dropping tear.

We studied in the garden and I went to and fro being fluid and resonant and dropping tears in a manner Emily considered totally unnecessary. Mine was the plodding method. I memorized with difficulty but once acquired, I pointed out with pride, "a thing was there to stick." Emily, I was shocked to discover, was an eleventh hour worker. With the same attitude she had in regard to trains, she saw no sense starting in to work until the morning of her lesson. She was, to use a theatrical term, a "lightning study" and would have been the mainstay of the sort of stock company which used to change their bill twice a week, for she could memorize anything in a flash and forget it in a similar flash. It was the only way she could do it, she said, for the short-est time she had in which to retain something, the better she could remember it.

The day of her first lesson, she rushed into the garden and started whipping through the "Nuit de Mai" two hours before she was due at Monsieur Dehelly's. I told her se-verely she had no right to go there so badly prepared, she was not serious enough and I gave her a lofty speech on high ideals and honest labor. I must have been pretty poisonous, for in those days, my conscience was as flaming a torch as ever guided my New England forbears.

My lesson was an hour ahead of Emily's and not any too wonderfully I got through half "The Oak and the Reed." When Emily came in, I stayed on, torn between a congealment of fear over what Monsieur was going to say, and a dreadful hankering to hear her speak her piece. She started and got through the first page without a mistake. I leaned back in my chair, faint with relief. Monsieur said, "C'est très bon," which disappointed me somewhat. He was about to have her repeat the stanzas, but he was reckoning without the quick powers of our infant prodigy. Without a break, she spoke the next page letter perfect, and then went on to the next, on and on, through that Night of May which, as one recalls it, is a fairly interminable one. Monsieur said she was a serious and hard-working student, and Emily smiled with the fatuous modesty of the scholar who after burning gallons of midnight oil finds virtue its own reward. My reaction was one of sudden frustration and rage. I glared at her and hissed in English, "I could hit you!" And now that I look back on it, I still think it was brutally unfair.

Maybe it was the sense of frustration which spurred me into turning creative that afternoon, or maybe I was bored with the oak and the reed. (Unlike the Child Wonder, I had, in a week, accomplished only half my assignment.) But for my own diversion, I began inventing a sort of solo act about an American girl visiting the Louvre. I wrote it down, memorized it and then with a good deal of shyness, told Emily I had "worked up a little skit," and would she care to hear it. To my astonishment, she became almost lyrical about it and said I must do it for the family. But I said, heavens NO! They'd think I was only frittering away my time. Monologue wasn't theatre. Emily said she didn't know why not; why couldn't I elaborate this sort of thing and do it in the theatre? I told her not to be a fool and went back hacking at that damned oak. But I couldn't

seem to concentrate very well. Something Emily had said
had given me an idea and gradually I began to say to myself, "I wonder. Maybe some day I might do monologues
in a theatre."

We went to the Comédie two or three times a week, but
I can't say we always sat in Monsieur Dehelly's loge. Sometimes we splurged and bought *fauteuils d'orchestre*, sometimes we perched like barn swallows on the wooden seats
of the top gallery, and often as not, we balanced on a
strapontin, one of those horrid little collapsible seats which
let down into the aisles, making escape in case of fire
impossible.

Most of the plays were the classics. The National Theatre, anything but niggardly, would offer two whole dramas
at one matinée . . . ten mortal acts. We would get fairly
exhausted, but during intermissions would stagger up to
the refreshment counter and renew our energy with a glass
of porto and a few stale slabs of dusty pastry. Occasionally
there would be a modern drama. I remember in particular
Paul Géraldy's "Aimer," which Grace George did here in
English, because we were so moved by the poignant beauty
of Piérat's performance. To me she was one of the most
exquisite artists of any theatre, and I am grateful I saw
her, for she died a few years later. My great master, Jean
Hervé, was also in "Aimer." He had come back from his
tour, and I returned to take a few more lessons with him.

He and Dehelly on several occasions introduced us to a
number of their confrères. One day, they told us we were
to have the privilege of meeting Mlle. L . . . , an engaging comedienne whose acting was of such gaiety and delicate charm, one forgot she was a good deal older than the
roles she played. We must meet her, they said, not alone

because of her art, but because of her virtue. She was an inspiring woman of the highest imaginable ideals. She had lived with a man for thirty years without being obligated by marriage. When his wife died, he offered to marry her, but she refused because it might spoil their relationship. And they both nodded their heads in solemn wonder at such a paragon. But when we expressed a desire to meet a certain other actor, they protested in horror. It was not suitable for *jeunes filles* to mention such a person, although he was a great artist. He was divorced, and of course meeting him was out of the question.

We went to other playhouses, we even saw a variety show at the Ambassadeurs with Mother and Father, but carried away a somewhat disjointed impression of it, because every time the chorus came out naked, which was almost constantly, Mother said nervously, "Shut your eyes, dears," and leaned over to make sure we did. She didn't understand French any too well, but when the audience went into roars of laughter she said, "Don't listen, girls. I'm sure it must be awful or they wouldn't laugh."

The evening we went to the Grand Guignol, however, was anything but disjointed. It was a steadily mounting, uninterrupted horror. A beau of Emily's asked us to go. He said it was by far the most amusing thing in Paris and Emily said he must be right. I had never gone to the Grand Guignol and had my doubts because I knew it was "awfully scarey." That only made Emily the more avid. Her favorite pastime was to read detective stories, especially if she could eat pop-corn at the same time, and she was in a fever to go. There were three one-act plays. One was a comedy of which I have not the slightest recollection. Of the other two, one was about a mad doctor and a night in

an insane asylum, and the other was that blood curdler, "Au Téléphone," in which a woman phones her husband who is in another city, telling him of the breaking into her house and the approach, step by step, of a murderer. The playwright fails to explain why, instead of her husband, she didn't telephone the police, but at the time we weren't thinking of that. This was the final play of the evening, and we came directly back to the pension, our knees clicking a tatoo against each other in the taxi. We were wearing our white fur coats, but we shivered as if it had been January. The young man left us at the door of the pension, and we entered into a pitch black interior.

Mme. Griffe, with an eye to economy, had installed one of those illuminating arrangements whereby just inside the door, one pulled a chain and a light went on. Something ticked loudly like a metronome, then after not more than twenty seconds, the light went off and could be relighted only by groping one's way back to the front door, and starting all over again. If we ran like antelopes, we could almost make our room by the last tick, but this particular night we were so frightened by the horrors we had been witnessing, our knees could not pick up the required speed. Two steps below the second floor, the last tick sounded and we still had another flight to go, amid a darkness so intense you could eat it with a spoon. Emily and I clutched at each other simultaneously. We were standing insecurely on a narrow step, the impact caused us to lose our footing, and we rolled, a bundle of fur and jellied fright, all the way down to the bottom of the first flight. Bruised and shaken as we were, we couldn't find the chain to turn the light on again, so we started crawling up on our hands and shaking knees. At the first landing my propensity for imagining extra terrors in the dark came to the fore as it did in the Rouen Cathedral and I hit on the idea that if anyone *were* breaking into the pension at the moment, he would know there was no possible way of turning on the lights, and we would be at his mercy. We managed to reach our room, unmurdered, but we clung fervently to the classic drama after that.

Whenever Dehelly and Jean Hervé introduced us to their fellow-players at the Comédie it was as "young American artists of the theatre," to which we smiled deprecatingly, but made no correction. We almost started to believe it ourselves. It was therefore no great surprise when, one day as we were lunching at a modest pavement café, a young man approached us and asked if we would do his cinema company the great honor of acting out for them a little movie scene. We were quite stunned, but managed to bow and say we should be glad to assist with our art, all the time kicking each other violently under the table. The young man sighed with gratitude and told us to stay just where we were, the mise-en-scène was perfect. Then he piled about us a mound of very smart luggage, all quite new and bearing labels from almost every corner of the globe. Emily asked him what we were to portray, and he said just two cosmopolitan women. The scene, he assured us, would lead up to something else and we need not bother with any action, simply give him the atmosphere of two very chic world travelers. He trained the camera on us, and glowing with satisfaction at his perspicacity in singling us out, we gave him generously of our gifts. We described the terrors of a storm in the China Sea, the beauties of an Adriatic sunset, the magic of cossacks singing along the frozen Don. Movies were silent in those days, but we spoke lines for him in luscious throaty voices, and an accent difficult indeed to ascribe to any specific locale. He told us we had given a beautiful performance, and we lowered our heads in happy modesty. If we cared to see the film, he said, it would be shown in two weeks at such and such a cinema house, and he wrote down the name.

The two weeks seemed endless. When the night of our world première came around, we persuaded Mother and Father to go with us, telling them we had a little surprise for them. There was a feature picture of sorts, then some news reels and finally, to our suffocating delight, there we were on the screen as large as life, sitting at a café table, completely surrounded with enormous pieces of luggage, both of us grinning like apes. Father emitted a loud "WHAT?" and Mother began making her little cooing sounds. We saw ourselves going through all those dramatic bits of dialogue, the storm at sea, the sunset at Ragusa, but the audience was not vouchsafed these bits of information. Instead, there appeared on the screen a version of our supposed conversation which went something like this, "Good gracious, Ethel dear, from the look of your luggage, you must have traveled everywhere!"

For a quick second there was a frightening close-up of me leering hideously. Then came the words, "I'll tell you a secret, Madge darling, I really haven't traveled at all. You can buy these labels by the package at the American Express Company. Decorate your luggage, my friends, the inexpensive way!"

That was the only time we appeared in the French theatre.

CHAPTER 13

WE haunted the book-stalls along the quais and spent hours in the wonderful *librarie* near the Odéon, occasionally making carefully chosen purchases, all of them French, and for the most part the classics. I imagine we were the only Americans in Paris that summer who did not come home with a copy of "Ulysses." Then we'd drift back across the river to the boulevards and the exclusive shops of the art dealers. This was Emily's idea. She knew a lot about modern painting, and could hold her own in any conversation centering around Cézanne or Matisse. I didn't always share her enthusiasm. For all my being hell-bent for culture, modern art was a blind spot, and a little Laurencin or Picasso went a long way with me. I used to accuse Emily of "just pretending" she understood such esoterics, and she in turn accused me of being capable only of understanding "The Horse Fair" or Meissoniers "Last Cartridge."

I could be arty just so long, then I'd have to go buy perfume. Perfume was one of my passions and I used to like to think I could identify various brands, the way a connoisseur distinguishes wines. Emily liked it, too, and we would go happily from one shop to another, being sprayed with large atomizers which would have been fine on fruit trees. We always got ourselves thoroughly drenched before making a choice, with the result that when we later walked down the street, passers-by were apt to reel a little.

One of our favorite cosmetic haunts was Bichara's, where members of the theatrical profession went for their powders and creams. It was just a niche in the rue de la Chausée d'Antin. The walls were covered with autographed photographs of every artist who had ever patronized the place, from Réjane to "les Dolly Sisters." The products were excellent and even if they hadn't been, I believe we would have purchased them because of the label on the boxes and bottles. There, a gentleman with dark hair and moustache, attired in full evening clothes is dashing in hot pursuit of a lady, very distraught and clad in a white nightgown, her hair streaming out behind like the tail of a runaway horse. The gentleman has almost reached her, and with outstretched hand is just about to make a grab for her hair. Beneath this allegory are the words *Monsieur Bichara saisit la Fortune*.

A weekly point of pilgrimage, however, and very different from our visits to M. Bichara, was the veteran's hospital at the Invalides to call on one of the *grands Blessés*, a victim of the last war. He had been hopelessly maimed at Verdun, and was not able to sit up. To eke out his small pension, he made bead necklaces, chains and choke collars which I had helped sell to Americans for him the preceding winter. Emily and I sold some for him that summer and he was pitifully grateful. Slung up in a harness, he spent his days in the bleak ward of that barnlike mausoleum which was built for Napoleon's wounded and hardly improved since. But for a week out of every year he was sent home with a nurse to spend a *vacance* with his family. He told us one day that his leave had been granted, and then, with a good deal of

embarrassment, asked us if we would do him and his wife
the honor of coming out to their house for lunch.

We were deeply touched to be asked, and the following
Sunday took a train to the little suburban town. A small
boy with a pinched, serious face met us at the station to
guide us to the house. It was tiny but immaculate and set
in a wee garden with tidy beds, graveled paths and white-
washed stones. The *blessé* had been a gardener before 1914.
The mistress of the house came out of a delicious-smelling
kitchen to greet us. She was lovely to look at, with black
hair, wide dark eyes and a pale, copper skin. And she
seemed touchingly young. We had thought of her husband
as an old man, his body was so twisted, the lines of suffering on his face so deep. She must have guessed our thoughts,
for as she led us into the small formal parlor, she pointed
to a picture on the wall.

"That was 'mon mari,'" she said, "in 1916" and she
turned abruptly into the kitchen.

It was one of those awful wedding pictures, the bride
sitting rigid in a chair and the bridegroom standing behind,
holding her down by a hand clamped firmly on her shoulder. He looked like a small boy, round-eyed, proud and
rather scared. The banal little portrait made our throats
contract, but when we looked at the young woman in the
kitchen, she was composed and smiling.

Her husband, she said, was expecting us. He was in the
salle à manger on a high movable bed. And he was a very
different man from the sad cripple of the Invalides. His
cheeks were flushed, his eyes bright, and he was full of gay
talk. He thanked us for coming, deprecated modestly our
praise of his house, but said it was *commode*, and we suddenly realized that for this week he was a man of property,

a citizen of a community, not just a number in a bleak government hospital.

His wife slipped in with glasses and a bottle of wine. He

opened it and poured, and she passed us each a glass. As we were about to drink to our mutual bonne fortune, the small boy who had met us at the station ran in asking, "Papa, may I have a little taste?" and he leaned across to take a sip from his father's glass. It had never occurred to us that the child was theirs, and for a moment it was hard for us to steady our glasses. We caught the young wife's eye, and in her face was a look of stark tragedy, unwinking and set with courage and despair. But for only an instant. The next, she was smiling and drinking the toast.

The lunch she had cooked was something to dream about,—a soup of herbs and vegetables, chicken cooked in wine, haricots verts from the garden, and a salad *fatiguéd* to drenching limpness in a vinegar and oil dressing with a faint rub of garlic. Toward the end of the meal, we heard a roar of machinery and a human voice which roared even louder. "C'est mon père," Madame explained simply. In a moment a colossus strode into the room. He had a rampant crest of white hair, a complexion like Santa Claus and the chest and shoulders of Muldoon. He came up to us, bowed over our hands and said he had come to pay his respects to the friends of his *beau-fils*, and he touched the shoulder of the *blessé* as gently as a woman. The old man said he had time only for a glass of wine to drink our health. When this was passed him, he rose to his feet. He wished, he said on behalf of his daughter, his son-in-law, and his country, to thank us and America . . . was it true there were buildings there of fifty stories? . . . a most unnatural height . . . for our kindness and good-will. Was it also true that wine was forbidden there? But that also was unnatural, and detrimental to the health. He then offered a tribute to the two countries and a prayer that their mutual *sympathie* might deepen through the years to come.

The speech, if a little full, was impressive and Emily hissed at me, "He must be the mayor or something." He rose to leave, full of regret, but a new road-building enterprise needed his attention, even on Sunday. We thought he was going off at least to lay a cornerstone and said good-bye with a good deal of ceremony. In a minute, we heard the same deafening chugging and rattling of a machine, and a voice shouting above it, "Vive l'Amérique! Vive la France!" Then the head and shoulders of the distinguished old gentleman went majestically across the window. A smock now covered his best Sunday suit and he was driving the local steam-roller.

Not long after that, Emily and John Mason Brown went to Fontainebleau for the day. I don't remember now why I was not also along, and, if truth were told, I believe I was somewhat "peeved" about it. The moment they got to the château, they were fastened upon by a guide whom they tried their best to shake. John waved his cane at him and Emily turned upon him a torrent of French invective (her French, these days, had grown by leaps and bounds). But the guide stuck like a burr, and John, the plutocrat, tried the method of handing him a lavish tip, in return for which they were taken on an exclusive route through not only the show-rooms, but a number of places not usually on view to the public. It was a day of soft sunshine, the place was almost deserted and after a time they forgot the very presence of the guide. They were peopling those stately, beautiful rooms, and the ghosts were pressing in on them. One could hear the brush of their stiff brocade over the parquetry floor, and the echo of their quick, high voices.

They walked through an apartment where a faint scent of musk seemed to linger in the hangings like autumn smoke. The guide opened a long window and they came out on a private balcony. Below them stretched an avenue of pollarded trees, sun-drenched at the entrance, cooler and darker within, like a green tunnel, the end of which was buried in the forest beyond. They stood there, barely hearing the patter of the guide as he mechanically repeated his memorized page of history, until John, catching a name he had uttered, whirled around and in his enthusiasm started shaking the man. Seldom was a guide more amazed. "That's it!" John shouted, "Madame de Maintenon!" and he peered into his face. The guide who spoke no English, had nothing to offer in reply, so John resorted to pantomime. He looked about for a prop, then snatched his handkerchief from his pocket and draped himself in a swooning attitude over the railing, looking back languorously at the guide, who stared at him blankly.

"Madame de Maintenon!" John cried loud and violently, beating his breast to indicate the role he was enacting. "Le mouchoir!" and he waved it at the staggered man. "Now then! *Yoo*-hoo, LOUIS!!" and he turned to wave like Isolde, over the balcony toward the allée of trees.

The guide's face broke into a rapturous grin of understanding.

"Oui, oui, oui, Monsieur!" he said, "c'est ça, exactment!"

"And Louis, he went hunting," John continued, "clop, clop, clop!" at that he went into a prancing step on the stone floor, "all his court behind him." He spread an imaginary train, "But he looked back at Madame de Maintenon. 'Au revoir, chérie!'" and John rolled his head back over his shoulder, "'I shall return to you bientôt!'" and with a wave of his hand, he pranced the length of the balcony with a high-gaited lope.

The guide was spell-bound with admiration. So was a new party of tourists who had just come out behind him. "Isn't it beautiful?" John said simply, and walked dreamily back through the crowd.

When Emily returned that evening to the pension, I met
her with the delirious news that a note had arrived for us

from the great organist Widor. We had met him one week-
end at the Fontainebleau music school, where he had flat-
tered me to a point of fatuousness by telling me I had the
ligne of an artist. I had never before had my *ligne* com-
mented on and was not quite sure what one was, but I took

the remark as a high compliment. He now wrote asking us both to come to mass next Sunday at St. Sulpice. He was playing a Bach mass and would we care to come up and sit with him in the choir loft. We at once sent a *petit bleu* telling him how *émues* we were, and that he might expect us.

At the church, a *huissier* met us and led us up to the loft. The benign old man was bent over the keys of the great instrument. Seeing us, he beckoned me to sit beside him on the bench, saying, "N'asseyez-vous pas sur le sentiment." I had no idea what a *sentiment* was, much less of sitting on it, but I doubled my legs up under me and kept very still. He was old and frail, but he filled the church with waves of thundering grandeur. When the service was over, the master took us up to a room above the choir loft to show us a tiny white and gold organ.

"Marie Antoinette gave it to Mozart," he said, and called a boy to pump it. Then he sat down on the bench and began to play some Mozart, exquisite and precise, but in the midst of it, he paused. "No," he said softly, "that's not what Mozart would have played. He would have preferred Lulli." And closing his eyes, swaying with the gentle plaintive melody, the old man brought into the church the whisper of an air by Lulli which the boy Mozart may have played at the instrument the gay little girl queen had given him.

———————

This was one of the last "big moments" we had together. For summer was drawing to a close. Father wanted to get back to New York to start work on his new play, and Mother began drawing in her nets from all the antique shops. I spent a day at the hotel helping her pack and

Emily decided she would go out to Chantilly for the races.

She had never been to a race-meet in her life, but from the papers it was very evident that the *haut monde* went there, so she put on her best crêpe marocain, took her guide book in hand and bought a second-class round-trip ticket. She arrived there long before lunch (that was because I had engineered her taking that particular train), and as the races didn't start till two, spent the time in the château, which she enjoyed vastly, especially because there were so many places where one could sit down, which made sightseeing very agreeable.

She heard some horns blowing, and after thinking at first it was a fire alarm, realized it was the bugle for the opening race, so she left for the track. She found a table where she could sit and eat and at the same time watch the sport of kings, and this seemed very fashionable indeed. She heard people talking about betting, and that gave her ideas too. People at races bet, of course—it was like Monte Carlo, sort of. She paid her check and began wandering about looking for a "racing tout." She had read about touts. She didn't find any. She had an idea from English detective stories, you placed your bets in secret with furtive old men, and got into trouble from them later on. She was therefore quite surprised when she saw the line-ups at the Pari Mutuel windows, and gradually gathered that bets were taken there quite openly, with gendarmes looking on. She reached the window, put down a twenty franc note, and was badly scared not to receive any change, but more scared to ask for it. The young man behind the wicket, who seemed to know what horse she was betting on, which was more than she did, handed her a ticket and said, "20 for

Astrid," and a lot of mumbo-jumbo about where the horse had to be in order for her to collect anything, which to her was nonsense because she thought a horse either won a race or didn't. But she thanked him and walked away. There were some folding chairs on the crest of a slope and she took possession of one, although several other people, mostly men, saw them at the same time, and the competition was acute. But the location was superb. Directly below her was the track and beyond, across the infield and moat, the château. She sat there enjoying the view, watching the pennants dancing in the sun and thinking how it must have been when knights jousted, pennants waved, and ladies leaned over a balcony and tossed a rose. The fact that most of the château was built in 1880 in no way upset this pretty idyll. As she was thus musing, suddenly the whole hillside rose up in front of her and she could see nothing but masses of obstructing backs. Standing on the chair, however, she could look over their heads and she saw that a race had begun. It was so beautiful, she wanted to cry . . . the long, shining bodies of the horses stretched taut and close to the ground, the vivid colors of the jockeys' shirts blown out in the wind, and the drum-roll of hooves as the horses pounded past. It was the most thrilling motion in the world, and she would have liked to have it go on forever. Then a Frenchman beside her said quietly "Astrid," and she came right out of her fantasy of perpetual motion.

"That's my horse!" she squealed at him in English, of which he obviously could not understand a word, "and my twenty francs! I've won a race!" In her excitement, she leaned forward tiptoe on the edge of the chair which, being a folding one, did what was expected of it. The front legs slipped under and the back smacked forward smartingly against her rear. She was catapulted off into space and as soon as she reached the ground went hurtling through the crowd, down hill, like an avalanche, while the chair, like Jill, came tumbling after. She is under the impression that several people were slightly hurt, but no one was more shaken than she. Some men carried her back up the hill, set her on her feet, dusted her off and retrieved her hat which had rolled in another direction. She could walk, although it was painful, and she decided she would go back to Paris without waiting for any more races. The ticket, however, was still in her hand, and when she discovered it, she hobbled over to the window, though she doubted if anything would come of it—there must be a fluke somewhere. Two hundred and eighty francs came of it, and she almost fainted from shock and weakness.

No one else was going back to Paris at that hour. The station was deserted except for an agent who seemed amazed that anyone should want to leave before the finish of the races, and vague in regard to time-tables. He murmured something about a train in five minutes, but he doubted if she'd want to take it. She asked why not, didn't it stop, and he said yes, it did stop, but he did not know if Mademoiselle would find it suitable. And he fluttered his hands. Emily, who thought that this was the silliest thing she had ever heard a station agent say, went out on the platform to wait for the unsuitable train.

In just a minute or two it arrived, looking like any other train, and she limped hurriedly along, in order to be near a compartment door at the moment of *arrêt*, which by now she had learned was merely a sudden clashing of cars without any bother on the part of the engineer to slow down. Before the clash took place, she was not only in front of a compartment door, she was in the compartment. She had been lifted up and scooped in by a bevy of soldiers. The train was a troop train and would stop only on signal. The station agent, a trifle dubious about her traveling alone with the French army, must have given only a kind of half-hearted signal, for the train made only a half-hearted stop. But it was enough for the boys to spy her waiting expectantly there on the platform, lean down, and take her along with them.

She said they could not possibly have been nicer. With a twinge of jealousy at her good luck, I remarked when she told me about it that she was lucky it was not one of those "8 horses, 40 men" box cars, but she said no, it was a perfectly good 2nd class compartment. It was dreadfully crowded, and she said there was nothing to do but sit on the knees of one and then another all the way to Paris. She told them about winning the race and they all cheered. They taught her a song too, which, she said, was full of new words for our vocabulary lists. It was indeed. We looked them up in the dictionary but failed to find any of them, which made us feel that perhaps we had better not ask any of our French acquaintances their meaning.

Ten days later we were to part. We had planned to sail home together, but Emily received an invitation to visit some friends at Deauville and go on a motor trip through the château district, and I told her she'd be crazy to miss the opportunity. I was sailing home on our old friend the *Empress of France*. Mother had been a bit dubious about my traveling alone, but she became reconciled to the idea because, she said, with her own logic, I *had* had the measles on that ship, so it wasn't as if it were a strange one.

The thought that our trip was drawing to a close was a dismal one. During those last days we bought clothes and hand-made underwear, as we had planned, but it hadn't quite the flavor we had anticipated. There were the usual crises over packages which didn't arrive, and after they did, the usual panic over what we'd pack them in. It took five extra valises apiece to hold all we had accumulated, but they were not really valises. It is hard to say just what they were, except round, for the most part, and made to look like leather, although after a little use, they proved to be made of some substance like *papier-mâché* finished off with black paint and shellac. However, they cost very little and made us feel we were not buying any more luggage.

The day before our departure, we blew ourselves to a superb lunch at Prunier's, after which we went on a pilgrimage to say good-bye to some of the places we had loved best . . . the rose window in the transept of Notre Dame, the little garden of St. Julien le Pauvre, the tomb of Ste. Geneviève to thank her for having saved Paris for us, Manet's "Olympia," and the lights at dusk coming on up the Champs Élysées. We didn't weep, but we were awfully quiet. The thought that we were leaving it all behind brought a lump into our throats, and the feeling in our stomachs that we were in an elevator descending rapidly . . . not a gay little Paris *ascenseur*, but a big, grown-up, skyscraper one. It was the end of something and we both knew it. We would come back again but it would never be the same. Our breath would come fast and our eyes smart when the Eiffel Tower rose again in the evening mist, but that would be because we remembered it from these months. There would never again be a "first time." Our hearts were young and gay and we were leaving a part of them forever in Paris.

Printed in the United States
151878LV00007B/41/A